GREAT LINCOLN DOCUMENTS

Historians Present Treasures from the
Gilder Lehrman Collection

GREAT LINCOLN DOCUMENTS

Historians Present Treasures
from the
Gilder Lehrman Collection

———

with an introduction by Douglas L. Wilson
and essays by

DAVID W. BLIGHT · GABOR S. BORITT
RICHARD J. CARWARDINE · ALLEN C. GUELZO
HAROLD HOLZER · LEWIS E. LEHRMAN
JAMES M. McPHERSON · STEVEN MINTZ
RUSSELL F. WEIGLEY · RONALD C. WHITE, JR.

THE GILDER LEHRMAN
INSTITUTE *of* AMERICAN HISTORY

NEW YORK · 2009

This book and all publications of the Gilder Lehrman Institute
are made possible through the generosity of the Julienne M. Michel Trust.

THE GILDER LEHRMAN
INSTITUTE *of* AMERICAN HISTORY
19 West 44th Street, Suite 500
New York, NY 10036
www.gilderlehrman.org

© 2009

ISBN 978-1-932821-46-8 (hardcover)
ISBN 978-1-932821-64-2 (limited edition)

Table of Contents

Foreword

—

To COMMEMORATE the bicentennial of the birth of Abraham Lincoln, the Gilder Lehrman Institute of American History has gathered in this volume some of the most important documents associated with the man many regard as our greatest president. Lincoln has been of central importance to the Gilder Lehrman Collection since Richard Gilder and Lewis E. Lehrman established the archive in 1991. Over the years that followed they built one of the finest collections of American historical documents ever assembled, with particular emphasis on the founding era and the nineteenth century. Among its treasures are nearly 500 Lincoln manuscripts, more than 10,000 Civil War soldiers' letters, and many thousands of other documents relating to slavery, abolition, and the Civil War era.

Each of the documents in this volume is introduced by a historian who offers insight into its context and significance. The historians are a distinguished group. They include award-winning scholars, several former winners of the Lincoln Prize, and the co-founder of the Collection, Mr. Lehrman himself. Originally, each of these brief essays was published individually as a keepsake for the Lincoln Prize, which was established in 1991 by Mr. Gilder and Mr. Lehrman. For the past eighteen years, the prize has recognized the best book on Lincoln and the Civil War era with a $50,000 award presented annually.

In keeping with the mission of the Gilder Lehrman Institute, "to promote the study and the love of American history," this book is being presented to the public in two versions. The first is an elegant hardcover edition designed for libraries, institutions, and individual Lincoln enthusiasts. The second, published in paperback, is intended to make these materials available inexpensively to the widest possible audience of students and teachers.

For anyone who takes an interest in American history, in Lincoln biography, or simply in great stories, the documents reproduced in this book are bound to touch a responsive chord. For some, the most exciting documents might be the handwritten notes for Lincoln's stump speeches in the 1858 Senate campaign against Stephen

Douglas. Lincoln carried each of these manuscripts in his hat or coat pocket, and thus one readily imagines their close physical connection with Lincoln himself. Others will be fascinated by his exertions on behalf of black voters in Louisiana in 1863, or his support in 1864 for the Thirteenth Amendment ending slavery. For me, the most touching document comes after Lincoln himself is gone. It is the letter Frederick Douglass wrote to a grieving Mary Todd Lincoln in August 1865, which closes this book, a letter that marks the beginning of their personal, and our national, efforts to recover from an almost insurmountable loss.

As Lincoln begins his third century in American memory, we hope this book will help future generations understand and appreciate his unique contribution to our country's history.

JAMES G. BASKER
President, Gilder Lehrman Institute

Lincoln the Writer

===

BY DOUGLAS L. WILSON*

ABRAHAM LINCOLN is arguably one of the greatest of all American writers. One has only to ask: How many American authors have characterized the critical experience of their own time with comparable aptness and eloquence? Whose ideas on the vital issues of American history have proved more penetrating and durable? Or perhaps most importantly, what other American writer's words are so universally recognized or so well remembered? Perhaps more than those of any other writer, Lincoln's words and ideas seem permanently engraved in the American imagination.

Lincoln's literary leanings go back to his childhood in Indiana, where he was remembered by his neighbors and peers as a writer of poetry and essays. As he became politically active as a young man, he began writing regularly for the local newspapers. He got his start in elective politics in an age of flamboyant oratory, but Lincoln soon recognized that his talent with words lay in a different direction. Thereafter, he pointedly avoided the flowery mode of conventional oratory and cultivated instead a style of speaking that was plainer and more direct. It is probably not coincidental that most nineteenth-century oratory does not translate well onto the page. The great political orators of Lincoln's day—Daniel Webster, John C. Calhoun, Henry Clay—as well as the great preachers, such as Charles Grandison Finney and Henry Ward Beecher, could electrify crowds of listeners, but that power could rarely be preserved, much less enhanced, on the printed page. Like newspaper copy, these speeches and sermons were destined to lose their appeal and their command over readers. By con-

* DOUGLAS L. WILSON *is the George A. Lawrence Distinguished Service Professor Emeritus of English and Co-director of the Lincoln Studies Center at Knox College. He received the Lincoln Prize in 1999 for* Honor's Voice: The Transformation of Abraham Lincoln *(1998) and in 2007 for* Lincoln's Sword: The Presidency and the Power of Words *(2006).*

trast, we still read many of Lincoln's speeches and other writings not only as historical documents, but also for their verbal vitality, the enduring test of literature.

Lincoln did not enter the presidency in 1861 with a reputation as a writer. His abilities, in fact, were regarded by most national observers as excessively modest and narrowly political. But slowly, almost imperceptibly, that would change. After he had issued a series of remarkable public letters in defense of his actions and policies, unprecedented presidential letters that were widely read and discussed, it began to dawn on readers, sophisticated and otherwise, that their unprepossessing president was a writer of no mean ability. In fact, the distinctive public voice that was projected by his writing eventually became a tangible force in the public arena, so much so that by the time he was assassinated at the beginning of his second term, the absence of his writing created a silence that was immediately evident. In the years to come, the body of written work he had produced as president gained such prominence and acclaim that it would permanently affect the way Americans understand their own history.

All of this helps to explain why manuscripts and other documents from the pen of Abraham Lincoln are considered supremely valuable artifacts. They are sought after and treasured as personal mementoes of one of the world's great heroes, but they are doubly valuable in establishing an intimate connection to Lincoln's creative process and the consequential words and ideas it brought forth. For students and admirers, the chance to see and examine a manuscript written by Lincoln is the nearest equivalent to being in the personal presence of the man. For scholars in quest of direct evidence of Lincoln's intellectual engagement at a certain time or on particular issues, these original documents are the ultimate primary sources, the starting place, as it were, of serious historical study.

It would be hard to imagine a better illustration of the ways in which primary documents constitute the basic building blocks of history than the Lincoln materials in the Gilder Lehrman Collection. As the sampling in this volume indicates, Lincoln's writings took many forms: letters, public and private; speeches, political and ceremonial; legal briefs, proclamations, and messages to Congress. Not all of his literary legacy is in the form of finished works; some consists of notes, preliminary drafts, and fragments, all of which tell us much not only about the formation of his ideas but his habits as a writer.

The one-page fragment of notes for a speech on government and slavery, featured in this collection, was originally part of a longer work, now lost. Yet fragment though it is, it rescues a valuable expression of Lincoln's political philosophy. Because he was always associated with minority parties, and also because he was a principled politician, Lincoln was destined to spend much of his time and energy in opposition—to the repeal of the Missouri Compromise, to the extension of slavery, to the *Dred Scott* decision, to the growing disparagement of the Declaration of Independence as a collection of "self-evident lies." This fragment shows Lincoln on the other tack, eloquently affirming his core belief that democracy was a positive, progressive, and liberating force in the world.

> <u>Most governments</u> have been based, practically, on the denial of equal rights of men, as I have, in part, stated them; <u>ours</u> began, by <u>affirming</u> those rights. <u>They</u> said, some men are too <u>ignorant</u>, and <u>vicious</u>, to share in government. Possibly so, said we; and, by your system, you would always keep them ignorant, and vicious. We proposed to give <u>all</u> a chance; and we expected the weak to grow stronger, the ignorant, wiser; and all better, and happier together. We made the experiment; and the fruit is before us. Look at it – think of it.

Here on display is at least one of the secrets of Lincoln's success. To make something so prosaic as a philosophy of government clear and vivid in the mind of a reader is a rare talent, but to render it so concisely and in such a way as to evoke feelings of pride and approbation is the mark of a great writer.

[1]

The Sanctity of the Law: Lincoln's Legal Career

—

BEFORE HE BECAME PRESIDENT, Lincoln supported himself and his family as an attorney. For nearly a quarter of a century, he was a country lawyer, who frequently traveled for up to six months a year through Illinois's 8th Judicial Circuit, which spanned fourteen counties. He handled more than 400 criminal and civil appeals before the Illinois Supreme Court. Altogether, Lincoln probably handled some 3,000 legal cases.

John Ford's 1939 film *Young Mr. Lincoln* popularized an image of the lawyer Lincoln as a crafty, cunning backwoods attorney whose practice consisted primarily of petty civil and criminal cases in which he represented friends and neighbors. It is certainly true that Lincoln lacked any formal legal training, either in a law school or from a preceptor (a judge or an experienced attorney). He gained his knowledge of the law largely from reading an eighteenth-century legal treatise, William Blackstone's *Commentaries on the Laws of England*, and researching and arguing contemporary case law.

But Lincoln succeeded in transforming himself into one of Illinois's leading trial and appeals attorneys, and he earned a substantial income from his legal practice, as much as $2,500 a year. He often represented the Illinois Central Railroad, but on one occasion, when he billed the railroad $5,000, the Illinois Central refused to pay. Lincoln went to court and won a judgment ordering the railroad to pay up.

* STEVEN MINTZ, *for many years the John and Rebecca Moores Professor of History at the University of Houston, now directs the Graduate School of Arts and Sciences Teaching Center at Columbia University. His most recent book,* Huck's Raft: A History of American Childhood (2004), *received several awards, including the 2005 Merle Curti Award from the Organization of American Historians.*

As an attorney, Lincoln took all kinds of cases. Although he is sometimes depicted as a corporate attorney, a defender of bankers, manufacturers, and railroads, he actually represented a wide range of clients. Some seventy-one times, he represented railroads, but in sixty-two cases, he represented clients who had been injured by railroads. His practice included cases involving contracts, debts, bankruptcies, and deeds. He and his partners even handled 110 divorces.

Lincoln's most famous criminal trial involved the 1857 prosecution of William "Duff" Armstrong for murder. An eyewitness claimed to have seen Armstrong fatally strike the victim. But Lincoln used a farmer's almanac to demonstrate that the moonlight would have been too dim to allow the witness to see what he claimed to have seen on the night of the murder.

About thirty-four of his cases dealt with slavery and race. In one case, Lincoln defended a free woman of color accused of failing to repay a loan, and in another, he helped secure the freedom of a fugitive slave. But Lincoln did not invariably take what we would today consider the "right" side in his cases. In 1847 he defended a slaveowner whose slaves sued for their freedom on the grounds that they had been brought into Illinois, a free state, from Kentucky. In another case, he argued that a black woman and her child should be delivered to a client as repayment for a debt.

From an early age, Lincoln was convinced that respect for law, legal procedure, and the Constitution provided the only secure basis for social order. In a speech he delivered on January 27, 1838, to the Young Men's Lyceum of Springfield, Illinois, he argued that the gravest threat to American democracy came from "the increasing disregard for law which pervades the country; the growing disposition to substitute the wild and furious passions, in lieu of the sober judgment of Courts; and the worse than savage mobs, for the executive ministers of justice."

When he became President, Lincoln viewed Southern secession as a fundamental threat to American legal and Constitutional principles. The Constitution, he insisted, was a permanent compact based on the principle of majority rule. A Republican candidate won the presidency in a fair election; the Confederate states refused to accept the outcome. Even worse, the Confederate states had left the Union for the sole purpose of perpetuating slavery. Only respect for the sanctity of law and the Constitution could preserve the nation from anarchy or mob rule.

This brief letter, to an Illinois attorney who, like Lincoln, had been born in Kentucky, gives vivid expression to the qualities that made him an effective lawyer, including his wit, even temper, and facility with words. Written on November 2, 1842, just two days before his marriage to Mary Todd, the letter reveals the young attorney's concern about finances and supporting a wife and family.

[*TRANSCRIPT*]

Abraham Lincoln to James S. Irwin Esq., November 2, 1842.

Springfield, Nov. 2 1842.

Ja^s. S. Irwin Esqr.

Owing to my absence, yours of the 22nd ult. was not received till this moment.

Judge Logan & myself are willing to attend to any business in the Supreme Court you may send us. As to fees, it is impossible to establish a rule that will apply in all, or even a great many cases. We believe we are never accused of being very unreasonable in this particular, and we would always be easily satisfied, provided we could see the money — but whatever fees we earn at a distance, if not paid <u>before</u>, we have noticed, we never hear of after the work is done. We therefore, are growing a little sensitive on that point.

Yours &tc.

A. Lincoln

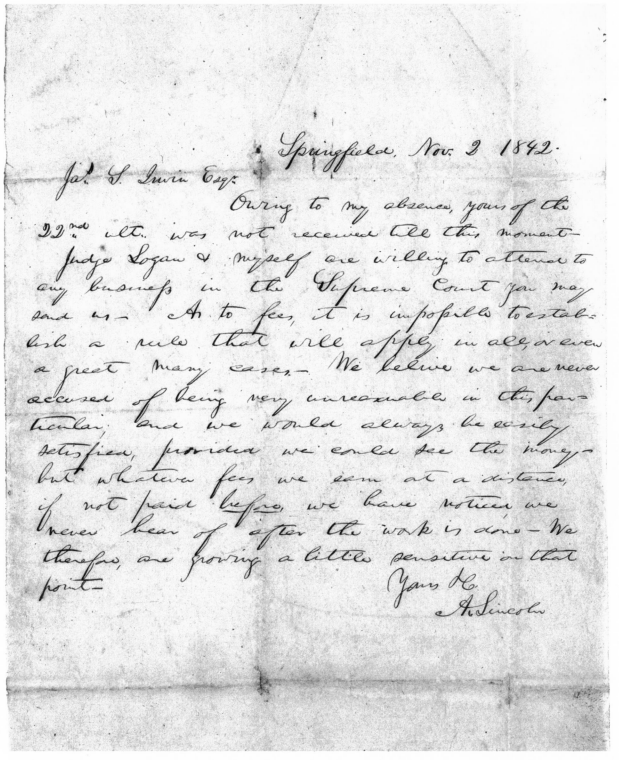

A letter from Abraham Lincoln to James S. Irwin, November 2, 1842. (GLC06256)

[2]

"This government can not endure permanently, half slave, half free": Lincoln and the "House Divided"

═══

BY GABOR S. BORITT*

T HE GOSPELS of Matthew, Mark, and Luke all proclaim, "a house divided against itself can not stand."[1] Living in a Bible-reading country, most nineteenth-century Americans knew that metaphor by heart—words that also made good common sense. Lincoln had used them as early as 1843 while organizing the nascent Whig Party in Illinois with his friends Stephen T. Logan and Albert T. Bledsoe. The trio identified the author of the quotation as "he whose wisdom surpasses that of all philosophers." But to demonstrate doubly that "union is strength," they also quoted another well-known source, the Greek storyteller Aesop, "fabulist and philosopher," who told the tale of "the bundle of sticks."[2] The moral of that story was simple: individual sticks were easily broken, but a bundle of them together held strong. Religion and classical learning stood shoulder to shoulder to demonstrate the importance of unity.

As sectional conflict in the United States increased, Lincoln thought more and more about the "house divided"—words abolitionists had long used in their fight against slavery. Being a prudent politician, however, he would not go as far as they did. Then, in 1854, the passage of Stephen A. Douglas's Kansas-Nebraska Act opened the West to the possible expansion of slavery and threw the American political system into turmoil. His passions aroused, Lincoln ran for the U.S. Senate, lost, and, distressed at what was taking place around him, confessed to a Kentucky

───────

*GABOR S. BORITT *is the Robert C. Fluhrer Professor of Civil War Studies and Director of the Civil War Institute at Gettysburg College. His many books include* Lincoln and the Economics of the American Dream *(1978) and* The Gettysburg Gospel: The Lincoln Speech that Nobody Knows *(2006).*

Abraham Lincoln (LEFT) during the 1858 campaign for the U.S. Senate. Stephen A. Douglas (RIGHT), here depicted c.1860, was Lincoln's rival for 20 years before the U.S. Senate campaign of 1858 and the presidential campaign of 1860. (GLC00590 & 05111.01.0286)

friend, a Congressman turned professor: "'Can we, as a nation, continue, together *permanently—forever*—half slave, and half free?' The problem is too mighty for me. May God, in his mercy, superintend the solution."[3]

This he wrote in a private letter in 1855. During the following year he appears to have spoken publicly along like lines, but the press took no great notice.[4] It was another year before Lincoln felt ready to think about saying the same thing in a way that would be really heard. By then the fight over slavery in Kansas had become so ugly that some called it a civil war; the government seemed to be forcing the institution widely despised by northerners onto Kansas; and in the *Dred Scott* decision, the Supreme Court had declared that black people could not be citizens of the United States. Lincoln feared that the next step would be forcing slavery into the free states. The future looked bleak for African Americans, and so for the country.

Lincoln believed that some northern politicians were plotting to help an aggressive slavocracy and that his nemesis, Illinois Senator Stephen A. Douglas, stood at the forefront of the effort. Even some Republicans began to back down from their stance against the extension of slavery and move toward Douglas's philosophy of popular sovereignty, a doctrine that could allow the continued growth of the American "cancer."[5] A crisis was at hand.

As a man of principle, Lincoln saw no middle ground on the slavery issue. The conflict represented, as he would soon say, "the eternal struggle between . . . right and wrong—throughout the world."[6] As a practical politician he knew Douglas had to be stopped. Finally, in the winter of 1857-58, Lincoln sat down and wrote what had been brewing in him for years.

> "A house divided against itself can not stand."
> I believe this government can not endure permanently, half slave, half free.[7]

Here it was on paper. Stark. Historic.

Lincoln was making careful notes for a firm public statement, as was his habit. These notes, saved by an accident of history and never intended for publication, represent a turning point in Lincoln's thought that would have been lost otherwise. The Illinois Republican knew that he was preparing a statement that would be heard around the country. We do not know whether he had any inkling that he was about to utter some of the most memorable words in American history.

The occasion to use his notes in public came in the summer of 1858, when he accepted the nomination of his party for Douglas's seat in the U.S. Senate.

> Mr. PRESIDENT and Gentlemen of the Convention.
> If we could first know *where* we are, and *whither* we are tending, we could then better judge *what* to do, and *how* to do it. . . .
> "A house divided against itself cannot stand."
> I believe this government cannot endure, permanently half *slave* and half *free*."[8]

This was the strongest, the most far-reaching public statement about slavery ever made by an important Republican leader. Although Lincoln denied radical intent,[9] that is what Americans heard. And in the weeks that followed, he repeated his words again and again, making it clear that his statement had been "carefully prepared."[10]

When Douglas attacked his argument, Lincoln could respond with humor: did the Senator think that a divided house would stand? Lincoln might add that he merely quoted the Scriptures: did the Senator wish to attack that—make war upon those words "as Satan does upon the Bible?"[11] Audiences laughed at that thought. But in all seriousness Lincoln also explained that slavery was the only institution that had ever threatened the American republic. There was no way around the problem. The evil had to be confronted.[12]

"A house divided against itself can not stand." Lincoln proclaimed a painful truth. He lost the Senate race to Douglas but two years later reached the Presidency. By telling the truth he helped end the division of the nation. Before that could happen, however, there would be a civil war—the worst disaster and greatest triumph of American history. The cost would be very high, but in the end the house would no longer be divided. After Lincoln, the house—the United States—would be "forever free."

NOTES

1. Matthew, 12:25; Mark, 3:25; Luke, 11:17.

2. Campaign Circular from Whig Committee, March 4, 1843, *The Collected Works of Abraham Lincoln*, ed. Roy P. Basler, 9 vols. (New Brunswick, NJ: Rutgers University Press, 1953-55), 1: 315. All three men signed the document and, though included in the definitive edition of Lincoln's works, its authorship is not entirely certain. Logan was Lincoln's senior law partner, and Bledsoe, also a lawyer, among other things, later became Assistant Secretary of War in the Confederacy.

3. Abraham Lincoln to George Robertson, August 15, 1855, *Collected Works*, 2: 318.

4. Don E. Fehrenbacher, *Prelude to Greatness: Lincoln in the 1850's* (Stanford: Stanford University Press, 1962), 91n.

5. Lincoln used the term to describe slavery. Speech at Peoria, Ill., October 16, 1854, *Collected Works*, 2: 274; Seventh and Last Debate with Stephen A. Douglas at Alton, Ill., October 15, 1858, *Collected Works*, 3: 313.

6. Seventh and Last Debate with Stephen A. Douglas at Alton, Ill., October 15, 1858, *Collected Works*, 3: 315.

7. "House Divided" speech fragment [c. December 1857], The Gilder Lehrman Collection, on deposit at the New-York Historical Society (GLC02533). This is the first time Lincoln used the metaphor in writing in reference to slavery and freedom. Basler, in *Collected Works*, 2: 452-53, having had no access to the Lincoln manuscript, used a variant text from John G. Nicolay and John Hay, eds., *The Complete Works of Abraham Lincoln*. 10 vols. (New York: Tandy, 1905), 4: 233-34.

8. "A House Divided," Speech at Springfield, Ill., June 16, 1858, *Collected Works*, 2: 461.

9. Abraham Lincoln to John L. Scripps, June 23, 1858, *Collected Works*, 2: 471.

10. Speech at Chicago, Ill., July 10, 1858, *Collected Works*, 2: 491. And see, in *Collected Works*, Speech at Springfield, Ill., July 17, 1858, 2: 513; First Debate with Stephen A. Douglas at Ottawa, Ill., August 21, 1858, 3: 17-8; Second Debate with Stephen A. Douglas at Freeport, Ill., August 27, 1858, 3: 72-3; Speech at Carlinville, Ill., August 31, 1858, 3: 78; Speeches at Clinton, Ill., September 2, 1858, 3: 82; Speech at Bloomington, Ill., September 4, 1858, 3: 86; Third Debate with Stephen A. Douglas at Jonesboro, Ill., September 15, 1858, 3: 120, 121; Seventh and Last Debate with Stephen A. Douglas at Alton, Ill., October 15, 1858, 3: 305, 309; Speech at Columbus, Ohio, September 16, 1859, 3: 407; Speech at Cincinnati, Ohio, September 17, 1859, 3: 438; Speech at Indianapolis, Ind., September 19, 1859, 3: 464.

11. Seventh and Last Debate with Stephen A. Douglas at Alton, Ill., October 15, 1858, *Collected Works*, 3: 305.

12. See note 10.

[*TRANSCRIPT*]

Lincoln's notes for the "House Divided" speech, c. December 1857.

Why, Kansas is neither the <u>whole</u>, nor a <u>tithe</u> of the real question.

"A house divided against itself can not stand"

I believe this government can not endure permanently, half slave, and half free.

I expressed this belief a year ago; and subsequent developments have but confirmed me.

I do not expect the Union to be dissolved. I do not expect the house to fall; but I <u>do</u> expect it will cease to be divided. It will become <u>all</u> one thing, or <u>all</u> the other. Either the opponents of slavery will arrest the further spread of it, and put it in course of ultimate extinction; or its advocates will push it forward till it shall become alike lawfull in <u>all</u> the states, old, as well as new. Do you doubt it? Study the Dred Scott decision, and then see, how little, even now, remains to be done.

That decision may be reduced to three points. The first is, that a negro can not be a citizen. That point is made in order to deprive the negro in every possible event, of the benefit of that provision of the U.S constitution which declares that: "The <u>citizens</u> of each State shall be entitled to all previleges and immunities of citizens in the several States."

The second point is, that the U.S constitution protects slavery, as property, in all the U.S. territories, and that neither congress, nor the people of the territories, nor any other power, can prohibit it, at any time prior to the formation of State constitutions.

This point is made, in order that the territories may safely be filled up with slaves, <u>before</u> the formation of State constitutions, and thereby to embarrass the free state [*not included in GLC document:* sentiment, and enhance the chances of slave constitutions being adopted.

The third point decided is that the voluntary bringing of Dred Scott into Illinois by his master, and holding him here a long time as a slave, did not operate his emancipation – did not make him free.]

Why, Kansas is neither the whole, nor a tithe of the real question—

"A house divided against itself can not stand."

I believe this government can not endure permanently, half slave, and half free—

I expressed this belief a year ago; and subsequent developements have but confirmed me.

I do not expect the Union to be dissolved— I do not expect the house to fall; but I do expect it will cease to be divided— It will become all one thing, or all the other— Either the opponents of slavery will arrest the further spread of it, and put it in course of ultimate extinction; or its advocates will push it forward till it shall become alike lawful in all the states, old, as well as new— Do you doubt it? Study the Dred Scott decision, and then see, how little, even now, remains to be done—

That decision may be reduced to three points— The first is, that a negro can not be a citizen— That point is made in order to deprive the negro in every possible event, of the benefit of that provision of the U. S Constitution which declares that; "The citizens of each State shall be entitled to all previleges and immunities of citizens in the several States"

The second point is, that the U. S constitution protects slavery, as property, in all the U. S. territories, and that neither congress, nor the people of the territories, nor any other power, can prohibit it, at any time prior to the formation of State constitutions—

This point is made, in order that the territories may safely be filled up with slaves, before the formation of State constitutions, and thereby to embarass the free state

Abraham Lincoln's notes for a speech on the "House Divided," c. December 1857. (GLC02533)

[3]

"To give all a chance": Lincoln, Abolition, and Economic Freedom

BY LEWIS E. LEHRMAN*

T O READ CAREFULLY the Lincoln economic parable of the ant (reprinted here) suggests a lost truth about our sixteenth president: during most of Abraham Lincoln's political career he focused not on anti-slavery but on economic policy. Yet anti-slavery and economic policy, in his worldview, were tightly linked. As Lincoln explained, slavery was grounded in coercion. It was, and is, an involuntary economic exchange of labor. In commercial terms, slavery is theft: "The ant, who has toiled and dragged a crumb to his nest, will furiously defend the fruit of his labor, against whatever robber assails him . . . the most dumb and stupid slave, that ever toiled for a master, does constantly <u>know</u> that he is wronged."[1] Slavery differs from free labor as a beast does from a man. Thus Lincoln assailed slavery not only on moral grounds but also on economic principle. This principle, he asserted, is a truth "made so plain by our good Father in Heaven, that all <u>feel</u> and <u>understand</u> it, even down to brutes and creeping insects."[2] We must not be misled by Lincoln's simple metaphors, for one of the profound strengths of Lincoln's political philosophy was his self-taught and masterful grasp of economic theory, more sophisticated than that of any President before or since. This is, I think, an inescapable conclusion from any careful study of Lincoln's collected writings, speeches and state papers.

Although Lincoln's nationalist economics were unmistakably Hamiltonian in policy, we still hear in his speeches the echoes of Thomas Jefferson's Declaration of Independence. On his way to Washington in early 1861, he declared in Philadelphia,

*LEWIS E. LEHRMAN *is Co-chairman of the Gilder Lehrman Institute of American History and co-founder of the Lincoln Prize. His book,* Lincoln at Peoria: The Turning Point, *was published in 2008.*

[14]

"I have never had a feeling politically that did not spring from the sentiments embodied in the Declaration of Independence."[3] "Most governments have been based, practically, on the denial of the equal rights of men," he had written earlier. "Ours began, by affirming those rights."[4] But only free labor can exercise equal rights. Lincoln's reaffirmation of this principle at Gettysburg in 1863 evoked "a new birth of freedom." At Gettysburg he insisted that America—despite the flaw of slavery, accepted in order to establish the Constitution—had been "dedicated to the proposition that all men are created equal."[5] One year later, combining the ideas of the great adversaries of the early republic—Alexander Hamilton and Thomas Jefferson—President Lincoln explained to Ohio soldiers visiting the White House that the Civil War itself was a struggle to create "an open field and a fair chance for your industry, enterprise and intelligence; that you may all have equal privileges in the race of life."[6] Then came the Emancipation and Civil Rights Amendments—the Thirteenth, Fourteenth and Fifteenth Amendments to the Constitution.

From time immemorial, America has struggled to be different from other nations. Bound together neither by race and blood, nor by ancestral territory, Americans inherit but a single patrimony: equality under the law and equality of opportunity. That Abraham Lincoln's equality was equality of opportunity cannot be denied. "I think the authors of that notable instrument [the Declaration of Independence] intended to include all men, but they did not intend to declare all men equal in all respects. They did not mean to say all were equal in color, size, intellect, moral developments, or social capacity. They defined with tolerable distinctness, in what respects they did consider all men created equal—equal in 'certain inalienable rights, among which are life, liberty and the pursuit of happiness.'"[7] This is what the emancipator said; and this is what he meant: "We proposed to give all a chance; and we expected the weak to grow stronger, the ignorant, wiser; and all better, and happier together."[8] And so, to be stronger and wiser, Americans have ever been ambitious for their liberal democracy. Lincoln, too, was ambitious. Indeed, he was history's most ambitious nation builder. Lincoln's law partner, William Herndon, described Lincoln's ambition as "a little engine that knew no rest."[9]

Lincoln was ambitious to use government to good effect. Government, he believed, should enable men and women to develop their freedom, their future, and their country. In his earliest political years, as a state legislator, Lincoln urged that government should be pro-labor *and* pro-business. During the decades before his presidency, he advocated government support in creating canals, railroads, banks, turnpikes, a national bank—all needed to integrate a national market—to the end of increasing opportunity, social mobility, and productivity. Like the first Secretary of the Treasury, Alexander Hamilton, and Senator Henry Clay of Kentucky, Lincoln sponsored an "American System." As an economic nationalist, he advocated a tariff to give the competitive advantage to American workers and American firms, and to enhance American independence. As a sophisticated student of banking and monetary policy, Lincoln argued throughout his political career for a sound national currency.

His economic philosophy rejected the idea of necessary conflict between labor and capital, believing them to be cooperative in nature. Cooperation could, in a society of free labor, lead to economic growth and increasing opportunity for all. In fact, Lincoln argued that capital was, itself, the result of the savings of free labor. Wrought by the mind and muscle of men, the products of labor yield savings, which are then deployed as capital. Thus, it follows that people are the most important resource, not wealth. This proposition was so important that President Lincoln argued in his first annual message to Congress in 1861 that "labor is prior to, and independent of, capital. Capital is only the fruit of labor, and could never have existed if labor had not first existed."[10] (Even "the ant will furiously defend the fruit of his labor."[11])

Nineteenth-century echoes of Lincoln's speeches roll down like thunder in the twentieth-century voice of Martin Luther King, Jr. For it was Lincoln who defined the essence of the American dream: "There is not, of necessity any such thing as the free hired laborer being fixed to that condition for life. . . . The prudent, penniless beginner in the world, labors for wages awhile, saves a surplus with which to buy tools or land for himself; then labors on his own account another while, and at length hires another new beginner to help him. This is the just, and generous, and prosperous system, which opens the way to all—gives hope to all, and . . . energy, and progress, and improvement of condition to all."[12] More than one hundred years later, King called for the economic rights that would take African Americans one step closer to freedom: the Negro's "unpaid labor made cotton king and established America as a significant nation in international commerce. Even after his release from chattel slavery, the nation grew over him, submerging him. . . . And so we still have a long, long way to go before we reach the promised land of freedom."[13]

From his deep experience, Lincoln had developed tenacious convictions. Born poor, he was probably the greatest of truly self-made men, believing, as he said, that "work, work, work, is the main thing."[14] His economic policy was designed not only "to clear the path for all," but to spell out incentives to encourage entrepreneurs to create new jobs, new products, new wealth. He believed in what historian Gabor Boritt has called "the right to rise."[15] Lincoln's America was, in principle, a colorblind America. "I want every man to have the chance," Lincoln announced in New Haven in March 1860, "and I believe a black man is entitled to it . . . when he may look forward and hope to be a hired laborer this year and the next, work for himself afterward, and finally to hire men to work for him! That is the true system."[16]

In Lincoln's American system, government fosters growth. Equal opportunity leads to social mobility. Intelligence and free labor lead to savings and entrepreneurship. Such a color-blind economic system was the counterpart of the Declaration's color-blind equality principle. The great black abolitionist Frederick Douglass saw this clearly, pronouncing a fitting tribute when he said of President Lincoln that he was "the first great man that I talked with in the United States freely, who in no single instance reminded me . . . of the difference of color." He attributed Lincoln's attitude to the fact that he and Lincoln were self-made men—"we both starting at the lowest rung of the ladder."[17]

President Lincoln's political and wartime legacy has transformed world history. As a last resort, he accepted war to preserve the Union, and with war, to free the slaves: "It is an issue which can only be tried by war, and decided by victory."[18] His grim determination to fight on to victory was not imprudent, he argued: "The national resources . . . are unexhausted, and, as we believe, inexhaustible."[19] Without Lincoln's leadership and resolve, separate slave and free states might today compete on the same continent. There would be no integrated, peerless American economy based on free labor. But without continental American industrial power, which Lincoln self-consciously advocated, the industrial means would not have been available to contain Imperial Germany as it reached for European hegemony in 1914. Neither would there have been a national power strong enough to destroy its successor, Hitler's Nazi Reich, nor to crush the aggressions of Imperial Japan. And, in the end, there would have been no unified, continental American power to oppose and overcome the Communist empire of the second half of the twentieth century. Empires based on the invidious distinctions of race and class—the defining characteristics of the malignant world powers of our era—were preempted by the force and leadership of a single world power, the United States of America. In Lincoln's words, "We made the experiment; and the fruit is before us. Look at it—think of it. Look at it, in its aggregate grandeur, of extent of country, and numbers of population—of ship, and steamboat, and rail-[road]."[20]

Hovering over the whole history of Lincoln's pilgrimage, there still lingers the enigma of a very private man—the impenetrable shadow of his profile. We scrutinize Lincoln's character; but we see him through a glass darkly. So we mine his papers, sap the memoirs left by those who knew him, plumb his personal relationships. But he escapes us.

Surely we know about his humble parents, his lack of formal education, his discreet but towering ambition. But we wonder that—unlike the Adamses, the Roosevelts, the Kennedys, the Bushes—no descendants carried on his legacy of national leadership. Like a luminous comet, he had for a twinkling thrust himself before our eyes, the eyes of the world, there to dissolve into the vasty deep whence he came.

NOTES

1. Abraham Lincoln, Fragment on Slavery, [1857-58?], The Gilder Lehrman Collection, on deposit at the New-York Historical Society (GLC03251); also printed in *The Collected Works of Abraham Lincoln*, ed. Roy P. Basler, 9 vols. (New Brunswick, NJ: Rutgers University Press, 1953-55), 2: 222. This document is an undated page of a manuscript by Abraham Lincoln, possibly written as part of a speech given in 1857-58.

2. GLC03251 and *Collected Works*, 2: 222.

3. Abraham Lincoln, Speech in Independence Hall, Philadelphia, Pa., February 22, 1861, *Collected Works*, 4: 240-41.

4. GLC03251 and *Collected Works*, 2: 222.

5. Abraham Lincoln, Gettysburg Address, November 19, 1863, *Collected Works*, 7: 22.

6. Abraham Lincoln, Speech to One Hundred Sixty-sixth Ohio Regiment, August 22, 1864, *Collected Works*, 7: 512.

7. Abraham Lincoln, Speech at Springfield, Ill., June 26, 1857, *Collected Works*, 2: 405-06.

8. GLC03251 and *Collected Works*, 2: 222.

9. William H. Herndon and Jesse W. Weik, *Herndon's Life of Lincoln: The History and Personal Recollections of Abraham Lincoln* (New York: Albert & Charles Boni, 1930), 304.

10. Abraham Lincoln, Annual Message to Congress, December 3, 1861, *Collected Works*, 5: 52

11. GLC03251 and *Collected Works*, 2: 222.

12. Abraham Lincoln, Annual Message to Congress, December 3, 1861, *Collected Works*, 5: 52

13. Clayborne Carson and Kris Shepard, eds. *A Call to Conscience: The Landmark Speeches of Dr. Martin Luther King, Jr.* (New York: Warner Books Inc., 2001), 182.

14. Abraham Lincoln, Letter to John M. Brockman, September 25, 1860, *Collected Works*, 4: 121.

15. See Gabor S. Boritt, *Lincoln and the Economics of the American Dream* (Memphis: Memphis State University Press, 1978).

16. Abraham Lincoln, Speech at New Haven, Conn., March 6, 1860, *Collected Works*, 4: 24-25.

17. Allen Thorndike Rice, ed., *Reminiscences of Abraham Lincoln by Distinguished Men of His Time* (New York: North American Publishing Co., 1886), 193.

18. Abraham Lincoln, Annual Message to Congress, December 6, 1864, *Collected Works*, 8: 151.

19. Abraham Lincoln, Annual Message to Congress, December 6, 1864, *Collected Works*, 8: 151.

20. GLC03251 and *Collected Works*, 2: 222.

[*TRANSCRIPT*]

Lincoln's notes for a speech on slavery and American government, c. 1857-58.

. . . [evi]dent truth—Made so plain by our good Father in Heaven, that all feel and understand it, even down to brutes and creeping insects. The ant, who has toiled and dragged a crumb to his nest, will furiously defend the fruit of his labor, against whatever robber assails him— So plain, that the most dumb and stupid slave that ever toiled for a master, does constantly know that he is wronged. So plain that no one, high or low, ever does mistake it, except in a plainly selfish way; for although volume upon volume is written to prove slavery a very good thing, we never hear of the man who wishes to take the good of it, by being a slave himself.

Most governments have been based, practically, on the denial of the equal rights of men, as I have, in part, stated them; ours began, by affirming those rights. They said, some men are too ignorant, and vicious, to share in government— Possibly so, said we; and, by your system, you would always keep them ignorant, and vicious— We proposed to give all a chance; and we expected the weak to grow stronger, the ignorant, wiser; and all better, and happier together—

We made the experiment; and the fruit is before us. Look at it— think of it. Look at it, in its aggregate grandeur, of extent of country, and numbers of population— of ship, and steamboat, and rail-[road] . . .

dent truth— Made so plain by our good Father in Heaven, that all _feel_ and _understand_ it, even down to brutes and creeping insects— The ant, who has toiled and dragged a crumb to his nest, will furiously defend the fruit of his labor, against whatever robber assails him— So plain, that the most dumb and stupid slave that ever toiled for a master, does constantly _know_ that he is wronged— So plain that no one, high or low; ever does mistake it, except in a plainly ~~selfish~~ way; for although volume upon volume is written to prove slavery a very good thing, we never hear of the man who wishes to take the good of it, by ~~being~~ a ~~slave himself~~—

Most governments have been based, practically, on the denial of the equal rights of men, as I have, in part, stated them; ~~ours~~ began, by ~~affirming~~ those rights— _They_ said, some men are too ~~ignorant~~, and _vicious_, to share in government— Possibly so, said we; and, by your system, you would always keep them ignorant, and vicious— We proposed to give _all_ a chance; and we expected the weak to grow stronger, the ignorant, wiser; and all better, and happier together—

We made the experiment; and the fruit is before us— Look at it— think of it— Look at it, in its aggregate grandeur, of extent of country, and number of population— of ships, and steamboat, and rail—

Abraham Lincoln's notes for a speech on slavery and American government, c. 1857-58. (GLC03251)

[4]

"That glorious consummation, which my own poor eyes may not last to see": Lincoln on the Abolition of Slavery

═══

BY ALLEN C. GUELZO*

THAT MAN WHO THINKS LINCOLN calmly sat down and gathered his robes about him, waiting for the people to call him, has a very erroneous knowledge of Lincoln," wrote Abraham Lincoln's long-time law partner, William Henry Herndon. "He was always calculating, and always planning ahead. His ambition was a little engine that knew no rest." And in no other pursuit was Lincoln more ambitious than in politics. As a lawyer and Whig political organizer in Illinois, "Politics were his life and his ambition his motive power."[1]

But at the same time, ambition in politics was regarded with deep suspicion in Lincoln's America. Our experiment in republican self-government was still a fragile one, and without the artificial restraints of aristocracy or class, Americans feared that ambition could easily run amok. Even Lincoln agreed that, as the example of the Founding Fathers drifted into the past, "men of sufficient talent and ambition will not be wanting to seize the opportunity, strike the blow, and overturn" the American republic. "Towering genius disdains a beaten path," he cautioned. "Is it unreasonable then to expect, that some man possessed of the loftiest genius, coupled with ambition sufficient to push it to its utmost stretch, will at some time, spring up among us?"[2]

───────

*ALLEN C. GUELZO *is Henry R. Luce Professor of the Civil War Era and Director of the Civil War Era Studies Program at Gettysburg College. He received the Lincoln Prize in 2000 for* Abraham Lincoln: Redeemer President *(1999) and in 2005 for* Lincoln's Emancipation Proclamation: The End of Slavery in America *(2004).*

Lithographs of Abraham Lincoln and William Wilberforce (1759-1833), the British politician Lincoln invoked as a hero of the fight to end the international slave trade and slavery itself. (Library of Congress Prints and Photographs Division)

The question in Lincoln's mind was whether ambition always needed to be so fatally self-serving. Ambition, he would write years later, "within reasonable bounds, does good rather than harm."[3] What he needed was a stage on which to test the quality of his ambition—and in 1858, as the national controversy over the extension of slavery boiled to life, he found it in his challenge to Stephen A. Douglas for the U.S. Senate.

At the beginning of that campaign, Lincoln took the trouble to write out a note on the subject of ambition and its aims, the note which is reproduced here.[4] (We are able to date this fragment to the summer of the Lincoln-Douglas campaign because the manuscript was presented by Robert Todd Lincoln to the Duchess of St. Albans as a gift in 1892, with the explanation that it was "made in preparing for one of the speeches in the joint-debate Campaign between Mr. Douglas & my father in 1858."[5])

The text begins with Lincoln's acknowledgement that "I have never professed an indifference to the honors of official station." He had always been ambitious for political office and political success, and any attempt to make himself look otherwise

[**23**]

would "only make myself look ridiculous." But ambition could also rise to nobler levels. "In the republican cause there is a higher aim than that of mere office." After all, if ambition could be satisfied with "mere office," Lincoln could have had it by less risky means than embracing the anti-slavery movement.

The proof of that argument was in the historical pudding. Pointing to the British anti-slavery movement, Lincoln noted that the "mere" office-seekers had routinely opposed emancipation. This included emancipation's "open fire-eating opponents; it's stealthy 'dont care' opponents; it's dollar and cent opponents; it's inferior race opponents; its negro equality opponents; and its religion and good order opponents." All of these, Lincoln notes wryly, "got offices, and their adversaries got none." But thirty years after the triumph of abolition in the British empire, who was remembered? "School-boys know that Wilbe[r]force, and Granville Sharpe,"—two of Britain's most devoted and tenacious enemies of slavery—"helped that cause forward; but who can now name a single man who labored to retard it?"

Ambition on the part of its citizens is the mark of a society willing to allow talent and ingenuity to rise. But ambition must not, as Joseph Conrad once wrote, "climb upward on the miseries or credulities of mankind."[6] In the last speech of the 1858 campaign, Lincoln admitted that "Ambition has been ascribed to me." That was true, and "I claim no insensibility to political honors." But he was laboring for a greater end than "political honors." If slavery could be restricted once and for all by electing Douglas, "on principle, I would, in consideration, gladly agree, that Judge Douglas should never be out, and I never in, an office, so long as we both or either, live."[7]

Lincoln knew how large a role ambition played in his own character, and how indispensable ambition was to the success of a nation without titled privilege or "fixed condition." But he also understood how necessary it was to the survival of popular government that ambition become the servant, not the master. "The proudest ambition he could desire was to do something for the elevation of the condition of his fellowman,"[8] he told an acquaintance, shortly before departing for Gettysburg to deliver his famous address. And few who knew Lincoln doubted the sincerity with which he said it. "He had a desire of power," wrote Charles Zane, the Springfield newspaper editor, "but it was that he might in the use of it benefit his fellow men."[9] Ambition was Lincoln's "humble mite" as well as his "little engine," and it provided the fuel that led, against all his expectations in 1858, to "that glorious consummation" of liberty and equality for all Americans.

NOTES

1. William Henry Herndon and Jesse William Weik, *Herndon's Lincoln: The True Story of a Great Life,* 3 vols. (Springfield, Ill.: The Herndon's Lincoln Publishing Company, 1888), 1: 375-376; Emmanuel Hertz, ed., *The Hidden Lincoln: From the Letters and Papers of William Henry Herndon* (New York: Blue Ribbon Books, 1940), 120.

2. *The Collected Works of Abraham Lincoln,* ed. Roy P. Basler, 9 vols. (New Brunswick, NJ: Rutgers University Press, 1953-55), 1: 110-111.

3. Abraham Lincoln to Joseph Hooker, January 26, 1863, *Collected Works,* 6: 79.

4. Abraham Lincoln, Speech fragment on the struggle against slavery, [1858], The Gilder Lehrman Collection, on deposit at the New-York Historical Society (GLC05302); also printed in *Collected Works,* 2: 483.

5. Robert Lincoln to the Duchess of St. Albans, September 17, 1892, *Collected Works,* 2: 483.

6. Joseph Conrad, *A Personal Record* (New York and London: Harper and Brothers, 1912), 12.

7. Abraham Lincoln, Last speech of the campaign at Springfield, Ill., October 30, 1858, *Collected Works,* 3: 335.

8. Abraham Lincoln, Reply to John Conness upon presentation of a cane, November 13, 1863, *Collected Works,* 7: 14.

9. Douglas L. Wilson and Rodney O. Davis, ed. *Herndon's Informants: Letters, Interviews & Statements about Abraham Lincoln* (Urbana: University of Illinois Press, 1998), 489.

[*TRANSCRIPT*]

Notes written by Lincoln for a speech on the abolition of slavery, c. 1858.

I have never professed an indifference to the honors of official station; and were I to do so now, I should only make myself ridiculous. Yet I have never failed—do not now fail— to remember that in the republican cause there is a higher aim than that of mere office— I have not allowed myself to forget that the abolition of the Slave-trade by Great Brittain, was agitated a hundred years before it was a final success; that the measure had it's open fire-eating opponents; it's stealthy "dont care" opponents; it's dollars and cent opponents; it's inferior race opponents; its negro equality opponents; and its religion and good order opponents; that all these opponents got offices, and their adversaries got none— But I have also remembered that though they blazed, like tallow-candles for a century, at last they flickered in the socket, died out, stank in the dark for a brief season, and were remembered no more, even by the smell— School-boys know that Wilbe[r]force, and Granville Sharpe, helped that cause forward; but who can now name a single man who labored to retard it? Remembering these things I can not but regard it as possible that the higher object of this contest may not be completely attained within

[Transcript continued on page 28.]

I have never professed an indifference to the honors of official station; and were I to do so now, I should only make myself ridiculous. Yet I have never failed— do not now fail— to remember that in the republican cause there is a higher aim than that of mere office— I have not allowed myself to forget that the abolition of the Slave-trade by Great Brittain, was agitated a hundred years before it was a final success; that the measure had its open fire-eating opponents; its stealthy "dont care" opponents; its dollar and cent opponents; its inferior race opponents; its negro equality opponents; and its religion and good order opponents; that all these opponents got offices, and their adversaries got none— But I have also remembered that though, they blazed, like tallow-candles for a century, at least they flickered in the socket, died out, stank in the dark for a brief season, and were remembered no more, even by the smell— School-boys know that Wilberforce, and Granville Sharpe, helped that cause forward; but who can now name a single man who labored to retard it? Remembering these things, I can not but regard it as possible that the higher object of this contest may not be completely attained within

Abraham Lincoln's notes for a speech on the abolition of slavery, c. 1858. (GLC05302)

[Transcript continued from page 26.]

the term of my natural life. But I can not doubt either that it will come in due time. Even in this view, I am proud, in my passing speck of time, to contribute an humble mite to that glorious consummation, which my own poor eyes may ~~never~~ not last to see—

the term of my, natural life. But I can not doubt either that it will come in due time. Even in this view, I am proud, in my passing speck of time, to contribute an humble mite to that glorious consummation, which my own poor eyes may not last to see—

Page 2 of Lincoln's notes on abolition.

[5]

"In the end you are sure to succeed": Lincoln on Perseverance

—

BY HAROLD HOLZER*

IF THERE WAS one quality Abraham Lincoln believed essential both to individual success and to social advancement, it was industriousness. A child of the impoverished frontier who went on to take proud advantage of what historian Gabor Boritt has called "the right to rise"[1] in America, Lincoln expected others to share his ambition for advancement. As he put it: "I am always for the man who wishes to work."[2]

Politically, this meant opposing slavery and advocating full opportunity: the hope, as he put it once, that "the weights should be lifted from the shoulders of all men, and that *all* should have an equal chance."[3] Personally, it meant urging friends and relatives to pursue the unfettered path toward upward mobility. "Free labor," he insisted, "has the inspiration of hope."[4]

Lincoln occasionally provided such inspiration himself. When a school teacher from Pleasant Plains, Illinois, wrote in 1860 to inquire how best to transform himself into a lawyer, Lincoln's advice was simple and straightforward: "Work, work, work is the main thing."[5] Later, as President, supervising the vast federal bureaucracy, Lincoln discovered that not everyone in government shared his enthusiasm for tireless labor. When asked by a needy mother in October 1861 to supply army jobs for her eager boys, the new President was barely able to contain a newfound cynicism when he obliged with a letter of referral. "Set them at it," he instructed an army major. "Wanting to work is so rare a merit, that it should be encouraged."[6]

---

* HAROLD HOLZER *is Co-chairman of the U.S. Abraham Lincoln Bicentennial Commission. Author of many books on Lincoln, he received the second place Lincoln Prize in 2005 for* Lincoln at Cooper Union: The Speech That Made Abraham Lincoln President *(2004).*

Lincoln may have been thinking back to the period, ten years earlier, when his own shiftless stepbrother had proposed selling the family's Illinois homestead and relocating to Missouri. John D. Johnston was guilty of one sin that Lincoln could not pardon: laziness. "If you intend to go to work, there is no better place than right where you are," he wrote scathingly. "If you do not intend to work, you can not get along any where. Squirming & crawling about from place to place can do no good. . . . you are destitute because you have idled away all your time. . . . Go to work is the only cure for your case."[7]

Such was precisely the case with—and advice for—George Clayton Latham of Springfield, Illinois, a young man whose aching disappointments and unique relationship with the Lincoln family inspired one of the most rousing personal letters in the entire Lincoln canon. Young Latham was the son of Ohio native Catherine Rue Taber Latham and Kentucky-born Philip C. Latham, one of Springfield's early settlers. The elder Latham joined the county clerk's office in 1827, and within eleven years had built a new home in town. His name later appeared as a co-signatory on a notice for the April 1840 election of Springfield Town Trustees, further suggesting his emergence as an important citizen of the new state capital. Son George was born on May 16, 1842.

But then tragedy struck. On May 25, 1844, the elder Latham was hit and killed by lightning near the village of Shawneetown. George and his four brothers and sisters were left fatherless. But not friendless. The Latham house stood only a few blocks from the Lincolns' Jackson Street dwelling, and George grew close to the Lincolns' eldest son, Robert. Together, they attended the local Estabrook Academy, then, beginning in 1854, the preparatory school of the new Illinois State University, which held classes in a onetime Presbyterian Church called the Mechanics' Union.

Robert, who was a year younger than George, took the Harvard University entrance exams in 1859—and failed miserably. To prepare him to take the tests anew his parents sent him off that September to Phillips Exeter Academy in New Hampshire (annual tuition: $24). George Latham joined Robert at Exeter as a fellow student, and the two were soon rooming together at the home of Mr. and Mrs. Samuel B. Clarke (at an additional cost of $2.25 per week). They were allowed to live off campus and study on their own (a reform only recently introduced by the strict faculty) as long as they were securely in their rooms by 7 pm. It is not known how successful the two boys were at honoring their curfew, but Abraham Lincoln certainly found them as inseparable as ever when he arrived for a visit at the end of February 1860.

The Lincoln Family, *by Francis B. Carpenter, oil on canvas, 1865. (Collection of the New-York Historical Society [1909.6]) This family portrait, painted in 1865 after Abraham Lincoln's assassination, retrospectively depicts the family at the White House in 1861. Eighteen-year-old Robert, standing in back, is a student at Harvard. Willie (11 years old), sitting next to his mother, died in 1862, and Tad (8 years old) would die in 1871.*

Lincoln had been invited east to speak at the Plymouth Church in Brooklyn, an appearance that instead blossomed into his celebrated appearance at the Cooper Union in Manhattan. His stunning New York oratorical debut transformed him almost overnight from a western politician into a formidable candidate for the White House. With his round-trip fare already paid by his hosts, Lincoln decided to extend his publicity-generating stay in the East. He headed into New England to deliver additional speeches, and also to visit his son.

At Exeter, Lincoln was reunited on February 29 not only with Robert, but with George Latham. The two teenagers then accompanied Lincoln to Concord and Manchester, where the presidential contender delivered two well-received speeches. The boys were doubtless on the scene as well on March 3 when Lincoln returned to Exeter and spoke at the local Young Men's Working Club. The next morning, the three worshipped together at a local church. The boys may not have realized it, but they were bearing witness to a political and historical transformation. Within months, Lincoln would win the Republican nomination for President. Meanwhile, Robert would enjoy a triumph of his own: on his second attempt, he passed the rigorous entrance tests and entered Harvard.

Unfortunately, George Latham did not fare as well. He failed the Harvard entrance exams. The younger Lincoln reported the bad news to his father, prompting Lincoln on July 22, 1860, to compose the magnificent letter of encouragement that is reproduced here. The mere fact that the busy and preoccupied candidate took time to do so in the midst of his campaign gives the effort particular poignancy. True to tradition, Lincoln did not actively electioneer on his own behalf that summer. He remained in Springfield, but his days were devoted to answering voluminous correspondence and conferring with aides and supporters. At the very time Robert informed his father of George's bitter disappointment, Lincoln was working to arrange meetings with his onetime rival William H. Seward of New York and his current running mate, Hannibal Hamlin of Maine. Simultaneously, the nominee was struggling to quell a small crisis of false allegations that he had once visited a retrograde "Know-Nothing" lodge in nearby Quincy.

At just this time Lincoln was also under siege by artists who had been sent to Springfield to paint portraits that could be adapted into popular prints. The candidate invariably cooperated with such requests, requiring only that the painters work while he scribbled away at his correspondence. As it happened, on the very day he sat down to write to George Clayton Latham, Lincoln was also posing for Boston artist Thomas M. Johnston. In fact, Johnston was likely observing him at the precise moment Lincoln penned the Latham letter. That same day, Johnston reported home: "I believe no man's personal appearance has been so variously misrepresented as the Hon. Abraham Lincoln's. . . . Mr. Lincoln has a fine head and face the expression of which indicates an amiable disposition combined with great force of character." That "force of character" was much in evidence in Lincoln's letter to George Latham.

He began it by confiding that he had "scarcely felt greater pain" than on learning of George's disappointment, but hastened to insist that the young man "allow no feeling of _discouragement_ to seize, and prey upon you." Surely George would have another opportunity, and when he did, Lincoln declared, "you _can_ not fail, if you resolutely determine that you _will_ not." Above all, the nominee advised, "having made the attempt, you _must_ succeed in it. '_Must_' is the word."[8] Echoing throughout the letter was that Lincolnian ethic: "Work, work, work is the main thing." For George, it likely made all the difference.

Abraham Lincoln–Hannibal Hamlin campaign poster, 1860. When Lincoln wrote to George Latham on July 22, 1860, he was sitting for artist Thomas M. Johnston. Johnston's painting was used for this campaign poster. (C.H. Brainard, 1860. Library of Congress Prints and Photographs Division.)

That fall, Abraham Lincoln won the presidential election. In February 1861 he left Springfield forever to make the long journey to Washington accompanied by his family—and by George Latham. Robert's friend traveled all the way to the capital with the Lincolns, and stayed in the White House for a week following the inauguration, before heading back to prep school at Exeter.

Eventually, Latham returned to live in Springfield, where he was reunited with Robert in May 1865 for a heartbreaking event: the martyred President's funeral and burial. Two years later, Latham married Olive Priest and entered his father-in-law's shoe business. The Lathams went on to raise three children of their own.

George Latham died in his old hometown on February 1, 1921, at the age of 78, and was buried in the same cemetery where Abraham Lincoln had been interred more than fifty years earlier. Saddened by the loss of his old companion, Robert Lincoln confessed: "With the death of . . . Mr. George Latham, there is not now in Springfield, I feel quite sure, a single one of my old men friends or even acquaintances who might write to me."

But Robert's father had written—famously and inspiringly—to George Latham, motivating him beyond a potentially crushing early failure. One of Lincoln's most accomplished personal letters, this gem of optimistic correspondence testifies as eloquently to Lincoln's own perseverance, discipline, and uncompromising work ethic as it does to his extraordinary ability to inspire others.

One thing is certain: Lincoln's words had not been lost on George Latham. The young man took Lincoln's advice to heart, studied hard, and went on to pass his college entrance exams and enter one of the great American universities. But not Harvard; George Clayton Latham went to Yale.

NOTES

1. See Gabor S. Boritt, *Lincoln and the Economics of the American Dream* (Memphis: Memphis State University Press, 1978).

2. Abraham Lincoln, Recommendation, Aug. 15, 1864, *The Collected Works of Abraham Lincoln*, ed. Roy P. Basler, 9 vols. (New Brunswick, NJ: Rutgers University Press, 1953-55), 7: 495.

3. Abraham Lincoln, Speech at Independence Hall, *Life of Abraham Lincoln*, by Joseph H. Barret (Cincinnati: Moore, Wilstach & Baldwin, 1865), 838.

4. Abraham Lincoln, Fragment on Free Labor, September 17, 1859, *Collected Works*, 3: 462.

5. Abraham Lincoln to John M. Brockman, September. 25, 1860, *Collected Works*, 4: 121.

6. Abraham Lincoln to George D. Ramsay, October 17, 1861, *Collected Works*, 4: 556.

7. Abraham Lincoln to John D. Johnston, November 4, 1851, *The Life of Abraham Lincoln*, by Ward Hill Lamon (Boston: J.R. Osgood, 1872), 338.

8. Abraham Lincoln to George C. Latham, July 22, 1860, The Gilder Lehrman Collection, on deposit at the New-York Historical Society (GLC03876); also published in *Collected Works*, 4: 87.

[*TRANSCRIPT*]

Lincoln to George C. Latham, July 22, 1860.

Springfield, Ills. July 22.1860.

My dear George

I have scarcely felt greater pain in my life than on learning yesterday from Bob's letter, that you had failed to enter Harvard University—And yet there is very little in it, if you will allow no feeling of discouragement to seize, and prey upon you— It is a certain truth, that you can enter, and graduate in, Harvard University; and having made the attempt, you must succeed in it. "Must" is the word–

I know not how to aid you, save in the assurance of one of mature age, and much severe experience, that you can not fail, if you resolutely determine, that you will not.

The President of the institution, can scarcely be other than a kind man; *[p.2]* and doubtless he would grant you an interview, and point out the readiest way to remove, or overcome, the obstacles which have thwarted you—

In your temporary failure there is no evidence that you may not yet be a better scholar, and a more successful man in the great struggle of life, than many others, who have entered college more easily—

Again I say let no feeling of discouragement prey upon you, and in the end you are sure to succeed–

With more than a common interest I subscribe myself.

Very truly your friend.

A Lincoln.

Springfield, Ills. July 22. 1860.

My dear George

I have scarcely felt greater pain in my life than on learning yesterday from Bob's letter, that you had failed to enter Harvard University— And yet there is very little in it, if you will allow no feeling of discouragement to seize, and prey upon you— It is a certain truth, that you can enter, and graduate in, Harvard University; and having made the attempt, you must succeed in it— "Must" is the word—

I know not how to aid you, save in the assurance of one of mature age, and much severe experience, that you can not fail, if you resolutely determine, that you will not.

The President of the institution, can scarcely be other than a kind man;

A letter from Abraham Lincoln to George C. Latham, July 22, 1860. (GLC03876)

and doubtless he would grant
you an interview, and point out
the readiest way to remove, or overcome, the obstacles which have threatened you—

In your temporary failure there is
no evidence that you may not yet
be a better scholar, and a more
successful man in the great strug-
gles of life, than many others, who
have entered College more easily—

Again I say let no feeling of discouragement prey upon you, and in the
end you are sure to succeed—

With more than a common interest I subscribe myself.

Very truly your friend.

A. Lincoln.

Page 2 of Lincoln's letter to George C. Latham.

[6]

Lincoln and Disloyalty:
The Dismissal of an Officer in 1862

===

BY RUSSELL F. WEIGLEY*

NINETEEN DAYS before Lincoln wrote the November 24, 1862 letter to Major John J. Key reprinted here, he had ordered Major General Henry W. Halleck, General in Chief of the Army, to relieve Major General George B. McClellan from command of the Army of the Potomac.[1] In the month of McClellan's removal and in the immediate aftermath of the Antietam campaign, the President could readily have believed that a circle of army officers with McClellan at its center desired to obstruct the winning of the Civil War in order to enhance the possibility of a negotiated peace with the Confederacy that would preserve the institution of slavery.

Lincoln could the more readily believe in such a cabal because even today McClellan's failure to win a decisive victory at the battle of Antietam strains credulity. General Robert E. Lee's Special Orders, No. 191 of September 9, dividing his Army of Northern Virginia into two wings including five separate detachments, had fallen into McClellan's hands on September 13. Thus the Confederate army was highly vulnerable to defeat. McClellan dallied without taking full advantage of this intelligence coup, but when he attacked Lee along Antietam Creek on September 17 the Confederates had still not completely regrouped. It required the Hollywood-style arrival of Major General Ambrose Powell Hill's Light Division at almost the last possible moment to prevent McClellan from crushing Lee's right flank and cutting his best line of retreat to the Potomac to save Lee from disaster. If McClellan had not badly mismanaged the battle, Hill's arrival could not have rescued the Confederate army.

Repeatedly on September 17 McClellan had been on the verge of breaking the Confederate line. Little Mac failed to coordinate his attacks, however, and to throw

---

* The late RUSSELL F. WEIGLEY *was Distinguished University Professor of History at Temple University. He received the Lincoln Prize in 2001 for* A Great Civil War: A Military and Political History, 1861-1865 *(2000).*

in the reserves that he had more than amply on hand, so Lee could always shift just enough troops to shore up the threatened areas. Never, until the final days of the war, was there so sure an opportunity to destroy the Confederacy's principal army and perhaps to win the war quickly. But McClellan's conduct of the whole Maryland campaign from the finding of the lost order, and particularly of the battle of Antietam itself, was virtually a textbook model of how not to wage war. In the inevitably overheated atmosphere of a desperate civil war, even the most rational observer could hardly avoid suspecting deliberate subversion of the Union cause.

It is striking testimony to Abraham Lincoln's generosity and forbearance—and to his recognition that McClellan possessed a devoted following within the army and considerable influence within the opposition Democratic Party—that the President refrained from dismissing the general from command promptly after Antietam. For a month and a half after the battle, however, McClellan failed to initiate a serious effort to follow Lee's retreat into Virginia and invade that state, so that by November 5 Lincoln at last lost patience and ordered McClellan's removal.

During those five weeks rumors increasingly circulated claiming that certain Union officers were plotting against rapid victory. In late September Lincoln learned that Major John J. Key of Indiana, an aide-de-camp to General Halleck, had been charged with disloyalty by a fellow officer. Lincoln summoned both men to the White House and received what he considered to be satisfactory proof that Key belonged to the obstructive cabal. After Antietam had made the possibility of a hostile plot so credible, Lincoln decided he must make an example of an officer who had seemed, in Lincoln's own presence, to confirm the plot's existence. He dismissed Major Key from the army in late September. Lincoln did not reverse his action, even after the death on November 11 of Key's son, an officer in the 50th Ohio Volunteer Infantry, who was wounded at Perryville.[2]

As Lincoln asserts in the letter here reprinted, against the background of the loss of a son, his dismissal of Key could not be a mere act of personal animosity.[3] Lincoln's language brings to mind his earlier letter to Cuthbert Bullitt of New Orleans, written July 28, 1862, in response to complaints that the Union army was behaving in Louisiana in ways that disrupted the institution of slavery. To Bullitt, Lincoln also affirmed that he did not act from personal animus: "I shall do nothing in malice. What I deal with is too vast for malicious dealing."[4]

Lincoln affirmed as well to Bullitt that the very work too vast for malicious dealing was the winning of the war, "and I shall do all I can to save the government, which is my sworn duty as well as my personal intention."[5] Probably a major reason why

Lincoln had remained patient so long with the military shortcomings of General McClellan was Lincoln's belief early in the war that many Southerners had not really wanted to leave the Union, but had been misled by wily politicians into supporting secession. In that case there would have been merit in McClellan's thinking that if the federal government and the invading Union army dealt generously with the South, avoiding damage to private property, respecting the institution of slavery, and treating all Southern white people in a friendly, forgiving way, then the South would be drawn back to its old allegiance. By the autumn of 1862 Lincoln no longer believed that. The motives of the South were more complicated than McClellan's and his own earlier judgment suggested. The South would not be brought back by generosity alone. Harsher measures would be necessary to win the war, particularly the emancipation of the slaves, on which Lincoln had decided by the time of the Bullitt letter, and which he announced in his Preliminary Emancipation Proclamation of September 22, 1862.

It was implicit in that proclamation that the General McClellans and Major Keys had to go. The war would become harsher, the Union forces no longer hesitating to inflict hard punishments on Southerners when punishments might appear necessary. As Lincoln wrote to Cuthbert Bullitt, those in the South who lamented the Union army's actions against slavery knew what they could do to end hard treatment: give up the war. "If they decline what I suggest, you scarcely need to ask what I will do. What would you do in my position? Would you drop the war where it is? Or, would you prosecute it in future, with elder-stalk squirts, charged with rose water? Would you deal lighter blows rather than heavier ones? Would you give up the contest, leaving any available means unapplied[?]"[6] As we see here, the difficult personal choice of dismissing Major Key struck Lincoln as one of the necessary available means.

NOTES

1. Abraham Lincoln to Henry Wager Halleck, November 5, 1862, *The Collected Works of Abraham Lincoln*, ed. Roy P. Basler, 9 vols. (New Brunswick, NJ: Rutgers University Press, 1953-55), 5: 485.

2. *Collected Works*, 5: 509, n. 2.

3. Abraham Lincoln to John J. Key, November 24, 1862, The Gilder Lehrman Collection, on deposit at the New-York Historical Society (GLC00496.045.01); also printed in *Collected Works*, 5: 508.

4. Abraham Lincoln to Cuthbert Bullitt, July 28, 1862, *Collected Works*, 5: 344-346.

5. Lincoln to Bullitt, July 28, 1862, *Collected Works*, 5: 346.

6. Lincoln to Bullitt, July 28, 1862, *Collected Works*, 5: 346.

[*TRANSCRIPT*]

Lincoln to John J. Key, November 24, 1862.

Executive Mansion,
Washington, Nov. 24, 1862.

Major John J. Key.
Dear Sir

A bundle of letters, including one from yourself, was, early last week, handed me by Gen. Halleck, as I understood, at your request. I sincerely sympathise with you in the death of your brave and noble son.

In regard to my dismissal of yourself from the military service, it seems to me you misunderstand me. I did not charge, or intend to charge, you with disloyalty. I had been brought to fear that there was a class of officers in the army, not very inconsiderable in numbers, who were playing a game to not beat the enemy when they could, on some peculiar notion as to the proper way of saving the Union; and when you were proved to me, in your own presence to have avowed yourself to be in favor of that "game" and did not attempt to controvert the proof, I dismissed you as an example, and a warning, to that supposed class. I bear you no ill-will; and I regret that I could not have the example without wounding you personally. But can I now, in view of the public interest, restore you to the service, by which the *[p.2]* army would understand that I indorse, and approve that game myself? If there was any doubt of your having made the avowal, the case would be different. But when it was proved to me, in your presence, you did not deny or attempt to deny it, but confirmed it in my mind by attempting to sustain the position by argument.

I am really sorry for the pain this case gives you, but I do not see how, consistently with duty, I can change it.

Yours &c.
A Lincoln

[p.3] The within, as appears, was written some time ago. On full reconsideration, I can not find sufficient ground to change the conclusion therein arrived at.

A. Lincoln

Dec. 27, 1862

Executive Mansion,

Washington, Nov. 24. , 1862.

Major John J. Key.
    Dear Sir

A bundle of letters, including one from yourself, was, early last week, handed me by Gen. Halleck, as I understood, at your request. I sincerely sympathise with you in the death of your brave and noble son.

In regard to my dismissal of yourself from the military service, it seems to me you misunderstand me. I did not charge, or intend to charge, you with disloyalty. I had been brought to fear that there was a class of officers in the army, not very inconsiderable in number, who were playing a game to not beat the enemy when they could, on some peculiar notion as to the proper way of saving the Union; and when you were proved to me, in your own presence to have avowed yourself to be in favor of that "game" and did not attempt to controvert the proof, I dismissed you as an example, and a warning to that supposed class. I bear you no ill-will, and I regret that I could not have the example without wounding you personally. But can I now, in view of the public interest, restore you to the service, by which the

A letter from Abraham Lincoln to John J. Key, November 24, 1862. (GLC00496.045.01)

army would understand that I indorse, and approve
that game myself? If there was any doubt of your
having made the avowal, this case would be different.
But when it was proved to me, in your presence, you did not
deny or attempt to deny it, but confirmed it in my mind
by attempting to sustain the position by argument.

I am really sorry for the pain the case gives you, but I do
not see how, consistently with duty, I can change it.

Yours &c.

A Lincoln

Page 2 of Lincoln's letter to John J. Key.

The within, as appears, was written some time ago. On full reconsideration, I can not find sufficient ground to change the conclusion therein arrived at.

A. Lincoln
Dec. 27. 1862.

Lincoln's note written on the back of his letter to Key, December 27, 1862.

[7]

Lincoln and Emancipation: Black Enfranchisement in 1863 Louisiana

===

BY RICHARD J. CARWARDINE*

A S T H E P R E S I D E N T of a fractured nation, Abraham Lincoln faced no issue more perplexing than that of restoring the rebel states to the Union. Reconstruction during wartime was, he judged, "the greatest question ever presented to practical statesmanship."[1] It meant managing a complex of competing demands: working within the Constitution, squaring local and national political demands, acknowledging military imperatives, and respecting justice for loyal Unionist southerners, white and black. Each of these issues was at play in the events surrounding Lincoln's landmark letter to three Louisiana Unionists in the summer of 1863, reprinted here.[2] The document offers evidence that emancipation was for Lincoln an irreversible process, even in areas not covered by his Emancipation Proclamation, and that freedom for the enslaved was more than a means to a restored Union: it was becoming an end in itself.

From the outset of the war Lincoln thought hard about restoration. He initially expected the Confederacy's Unionists to repudiate the rebellion of what he perceived to be a self-deluding minority. In a perpetual Union, he insisted, secession could have no legal status; the rebel states remained under a federal constitution that gave the president, as commander in chief, control of wartime reconstruction policy. His duty was to nurture local initiatives toward restoring self-government and ending the rebellion. It was unlikely to involve any revolutionary tampering

* R I C H A R D J . C A R W A R D I N E *is the Rhodes Professor of American History at Oxford University. His biography,* Lincoln: A Life of Purpose and Power *(2003), received the Lincoln Prize in 2004.*

with southern slavery. Gradual, constitutional change offered the best hope of maintaining the political consensus essential to Union victory and a lasting peace.

Lincoln's early approach would eventually founder on the realities of broad-based southern resistance, the weakness of Confederate Unionism, and the failure of the federal armies. During the summer of 1862 Lincoln concluded that emancipating secessionists' slaves—bondage being an element vital to the South's war effort—had come to be one of the "indispensable means" of the Union's salvation. Invoking his constitutional power as commander in chief, the President issued a Preliminary Emancipation Proclamation on September 22, and a hundred days later not only declared free the slaves in Confederate-held areas, but also opened the doors of the Union's army and navy to the enlistment of African Americans as fighting men.

The Emancipation Proclamation heralded the death of the old Union. As the federal armies ate away at the borders of the Confederacy after New Year's Day 1863, they became agents of liberation for the slaves who swarmed towards their approach. Both conviction and pragmatism ensured that Lincoln would hold steadfast to his new policy, though for the first half of that year he had little to show for it. The Union's mood changed radically in the early days of July, following dramatic successes at Gettysburg and Vicksburg. Lincoln would increasingly describe his proclamation as an irreversible order, making explicit what previously he had merely implied: black freedom had become an objective of the war. "I think I shall not retract or repudiate" the proclamation, he told Stephen Hurlbut in late July. "Those who shall have tasted actual freedom I believe can never be slaves, or quasi slaves again."[3] It was a position he would reaffirm memorably at Gettysburg in November.

Lincoln's letter to Thomas Cottman and his associates draws our attention to the local conditions prevailing in Louisiana. Here in the spring of 1862 federal forces and a military governor had taken control of New Orleans and the neighboring parishes. Lincoln hoped the state's restoration might become a model for others. The presence in the city of an educated, propertied free black population alongside one of the most substantial white Unionist communities in the lower South seemed to offer a viable nucleus for building a loyal government. But Louisiana Unionists were divided along a conservative-radical fault line over slavery's place in the reconstituted order. Needing to hold together this coalition of proslavery planters and antislavery businessmen and workers, Lincoln was reluctant to see any local policy that would frighten off the conservatives, and even after issuing his preliminary emancipation order—which excluded the thirteen loyal parishes of Union-controlled Louisiana—he continued to offer "peace again upon the old terms under the constitution."[4] This, however, would

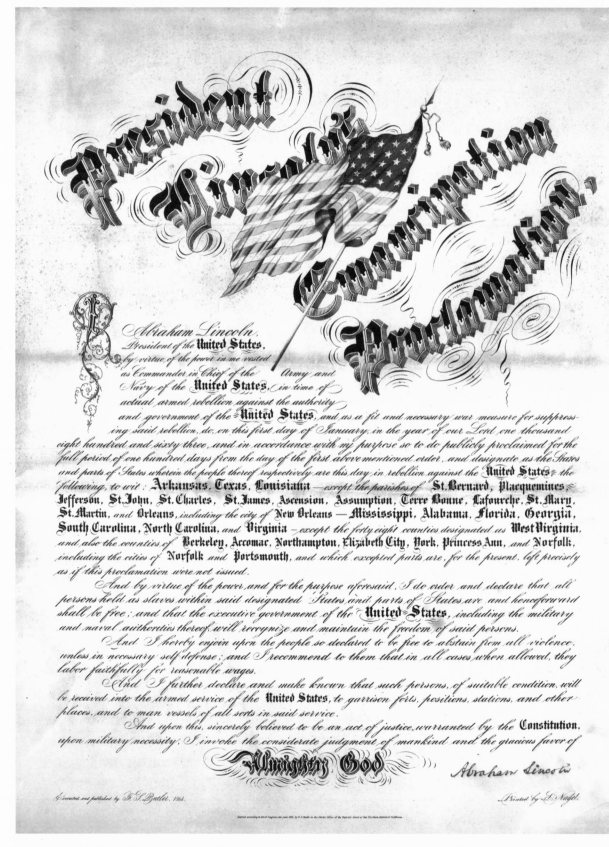

Lithograph of the Emancipation Proclamation, designed by a 14-year-old Californian and signed by Lincoln, published by F.S. Butler and printed by L. Nagel, San Francisco, Ca., 1864. (GLC00742)

depend on their moving swiftly to hold elections. A December 1862 vote in two congressional districts saw the return of two Unionist candidates, Benjamin F. Flanders and Michael Hahn. But radical Republicans, locally and in Congress, denounced the harsh "free-labor" regime which Nathaniel Banks, the commanding general, established in Louisiana to control the thousands of ex-slaves whose presence portended economic chaos, social confusion, and a threat to military efficiency.

Lincoln let Banks's contractual labor system stand. However, in the battle between Louisiana planter conservatives, who wanted to organize the state under the pre-war constitution, and the free-state men, the president's instincts and private encouragement put him on the side of the progressives. He also wanted a "bottom-up" movement, not a Washington-imposed one. From the spring of 1863 he let it be known, discreetly, that Louisiana's restoration would be linked to its organization as a "free state," one that had embraced emancipation. He quietly lent his support to the plan to elect a state constitutional convention that would abolish slavery. It was the pro-slavery opponents of the free-state men who would push Lincoln into his "first open, but indirect, indication of support for the Free State movement."[5] The planters sent a three-man delegation to the White House, led by the staunchly pro-slavery Cottman, to ask the president for "a full recognition of all the rights of the State, as they existed previous to the passage of an act of secession, upon the principle of the existence of the State Constitution unimpaired";[6] to that end they called for a November election under the old forms. Cottman judged that the President's position on the persisting *de jure* authority of the federal constitution within the rebel states, and his exclusion of Louisiana parishes from the terms of the Emancipation Proclamation, meant that Lincoln would be in sympathy with the planters' wish to see the state "return to its full allegiance" under the existing constitution.

Lincoln, however, was in no mind to fall in line. He made the delegation wait until only Cottman remained in Washington. His reply, designed for the press, explained that he was reliably informed that "a respectable portion of the Louisiana people" now sought to adopt a revised (that is, free-state) constitution: "This fact alone, as it seems to me, is a sufficient reason why the general government should not give the committal you seek, to the existing State constitution."[7] He did not go so far as publicly to endorse the free-state party. If restoration were to succeed, he needed to keep united the minority of Union men in Louisiana. But equally, he was not prepared passively to accept slavery's perpetuation there.

What Lincoln intimated in the Cottman letter he continued to spell out privately, telling Banks in August 1863 that he did not want "to assume direction" of the state's affairs, but that he "would be glad for her to make a new Constitution recognizing the emancipation proclamation, and adopting emancipation in those parts of the state to which the proclamation does not apply." Intimating his preference for a gentle evolution out of slavery, he continued: "And while she is at it, I think it would not be objectionable for her to adopt some practical system by which the two races could gradually live themselves out of their old relation to each other, and both come out better prepared for the new." Lincoln urged him to "confer with intelligent and trusty citizens of the State" and prepare the way for a state constitutional convention that would eliminate slavery.[8]

Having firmly told Banks to be "master" there, Lincoln felt he had to fall in with his commander's decision to hold elections in February 1864 under the pre-war constitution. Fears that pro-slavery forces would secure control proved unfounded, but the convention that followed the victory of the more conservative free-state men produced a constitution too cautious for the radicals, who attacked the failure to advance beyond the promise of immediate, uncompensated emancipation and to give blacks the protection of the vote. Lincoln, though, welcomed what he judged a huge step forward, one which gave the freedmen of Louisiana greater civil and educational advantages than the blacks of his own Illinois.

He continued cautiously to move onto the radicals' terrain. In March 1864 he urged Michael Hahn, recently elected as Louisiana's first free-state governor, to promote a new constitution that would confer voting rights on "some of the colored people," both "the very intelligent, and especially those who have fought gallantly in our ranks." They would, he judged, "probably help, in some trying time to come, to keep the jewel of liberty within the family of freedom."[9] Just over a year later, in what turned out to be his final public address, he offered a vision of the future in which at least some blacks—including thousands who had recently been no more than illiterate field-hands—received the political rights enjoyed by whites.

The Lincoln who had never doubted that African Americans were embraced by the principles of the Declaration of Independence, but who before the war had disclaimed any intention of raising blacks to social and political equality with whites, and who had advocated the voluntary colonization of African Americans abroad, was by the time of his death meaningfully pursuing the integration of blacks into the reconstructed nation as the civic equals of whites.

NOTES

1. *Inside Lincoln's White House: The Complete Civil War Diary of John Hay.* eds. Michael Burlingame and John R. Turner Ettlinger (Carbondale, Illinois: Southern Illinois University Press, 1997), 69.

2. Abraham Lincoln to E.E. Malhiot, Bradish Johnson, and Thomas Cottman, June 19, 1863, The Gilder Lehrman Collection, on deposit at the New-York Historical Society (GLC01571); also printed in *The Collected Works of Abraham Lincoln,* ed. Roy P. Basler, 9 vols. (New Brunswick, NJ: Rutgers University Press, 1953-55), 6: 287-289.

3. Abraham Lincoln to Stephen Hurlbutt, July 31, 1863, *Collected Works,* 6: 358.

4. Abraham Lincoln to Benjamin F. Butler, George F. Shepley and Others, October. 14, 1862, *Collected Works,* 5: 462.

5. LaWanda Cox, *Lincoln and Black Freedom: A Study in Presidential Leadership* (Columbia: University of South Carolina Press, 1981), 52.

6. GLC01571.

7. GLC01571.

8. Abraham Lincoln to Nathaniel P. Banks, August 5, 1863, *Collected Works,* 6: 364-65.

9. Abraham Lincoln to Michael Hahn, March 13, 1864, *Collected Works,* 7:243.

[*TRANSCRIPT*]

Lincoln to E. E. Malhiot, Bradish Johnson and Thomas Cottman, June 19, 1863.

Executive Mansion
Washington, June 19, 1863.

Messrs. E. E. Malhiot
Bradish Johnson; &
Thomas Cottman,
Gentlemen:
Your letter which follows has
been received and considered:
"To His Excellency
Abraham Lincoln,
President of the United States,
The undersigned, a committee appointed by the Planters
of the State of Louisiana, respectfully represent, that they
have been delegated to seek of the General Government a full
recognition of all the rights of the State as they existed previ-
ous to the passage of an act of secession, upon the principle of
the existence of the State Constitution unimpaired, and no
legal act having transpired that could in any way de-

[Transcript continued on page 54.]

A letter from Abraham Lincoln to E. E. Malhiot, Bradish Johnson, and Thomas Cottman of Louisiana, June 19, 1863. (GLC01571)

[Transcript continued from page 52.]

prive them of the advantages conferred by that Constitution. Under this Constitution the State wishes to return to its full allegiance, in the enjoyment of all rights and privileges exercised by the other States under the Federal Constitution. With the view of accomplishing the desired object, we farther request that your Excellency will as Commander-in-Chief of the Army of the United States direct the Military Governor of Louisiana to order an election in conformity with the Constitution and laws of the State, on the first Monday of November next, for all State and Federal officers.

With high consideration and respect we have the honor to subscribe ourselves,

> Your Obt Servts.
> (signed)   E. E. Malhiot
>   Bradish Johnson
>   Thos. Cottman."

Since receiving the letter, reliable

[Transcript continued on page 56.]

prive them of the advantages conferred by that Constitution. Under this Constitution the State wishes to return to its full allegiance, in the enjoyment of all rights and privileges exercised by the other States under the Federal Constitution. With the view of accomplishing the desired object, we farther request that your Excellency will as Commander-in-Chief of the Army of the United States direct the Military Governor of Louisiana to order an election in conformity with the Constitution and laws of the State, on the first Monday of November next, for all State and Federal officers.

With high consideration and respect we have the honor to subscribe ourselves,

Your obt. Servts.

(signed)   E. E. Malhiot

Bradish Johnson

Thos. Cottman. "

Since receiving this letter, reliable

Page 2 of Lincoln's letter to Louisiana Unionists.

[Transcript continued from page 54.]

information has reached me that a respectable portion of the Louisiana people desire to amend their State Constitution, and contemplate holding a Convention for that object. This fact alone, as it seems to me, is a sufficient reason why the general government should not give the committal you seek, to the existing State Constitution. I may add that while I do not perceive how such committal could facilitate our military operations in Louisiana, I really apprehend it might be so used as to embarrass them.

As to an election to be held next November, there is abundant time, without any order, or proclamation from me just now. The people of Louisiana shall not lack an opportunity of a fair election for both Federal and State officers, by want of anything within my power to give them.

Your obt. Servt.

A. Lincoln.

information has reached me that a res=
pectable portion of the Louisiana people
desire to amend their State Constitution,
and contemplate holding a Convention for that
object. This fact alone, as it seems to me,
is a sufficient reason why the general government should not give the committal you
seek, to the existing State Constitution. I may
add that while I do not perceive how such
committal could facilitate our military operations in Louisiana, I really apprehend
it might be so used as to embarrass them.

As to an election to be held next Novem=
ber, there is abundant time, without any order,
or proclamation from me just now. The
people of Louisiana shall not lack an opportunity of a fair election for both Federal
and State officers, by want of anything
within my power to give them.

Your obt Servt

A. Lincoln.

Page 3 of Lincoln's letter to Louisiana Unionists.

[8]

"I begin to see it": Lincoln the War President

BY JAMES M. MCPHERSON*

IN THE SPRING of 1864, three years into the Civil War, it seemed that the Union was finally in a position to defeat the Confederacy, taking advantage of the significant losses the Confederacy had suffered in 1863. For three years, Lincoln had been repeatedly disappointed by the lack of ability and determination of his generals in their pursuit of the enemy, but with the appointment of Ulysses S. Grant as general in chief in March 1864, Lincoln felt the Union army would be prepared to press any advantage to stop the Confederacy.

By mid June, Grant and the Army of the Potomac had been trying for six weeks to pry the enemy from its formidable defenses in Virginia at Spotsylvania and at Cold Harbor for a fight in the open where larger Union numbers could prevail. The skillful General Robert E. Lee had foiled each movement, forcing Grant repeatedly to attack those defenses at the cost of 45,000 Union casualties from May 5 through June 14. On June 15, 1864, Lincoln sent General Grant a telegram, reprinted here, in response to a dispatch from the general informing him that the Army of the Potomac had cut loose from its lines at Cold Harbor, Virginia, just east of Richmond, and marched twenty-five miles south to break the enemy's railroad supply route through Petersburg, Virginia. Grant hoped that this move would force Lee's Army of Northern Virginia out of its trenches to fight for its communications lifeline.

Grant's purpose in this campaign was not principally to capture Richmond, but to cripple or destroy the Army of Northern Virginia. This objective conformed to Lin-

---

*JAMES M. MCPHERSON *is George Henry Davis '86 Professor of American History Emeritus at Princeton University and a Pulitzer Prize–winning author. His book* For Cause and Comrades: Why Men Fought in the Civil War *(1997) won the Lincoln Prize in 1998.*

Abraham Lincoln, February 9, 1864.
(GLC07735)

Ulysses S. Grant, 1865.
(GLC00553)

coln's military strategy from early in the war. As commander in chief, the Civil War president performed several functions. The first was formulation of *policy*: the nation's war aims. On this matter Lincoln never wavered; his policy was preservation of the United States as one nation by suppressing this rebellion that sought to split the nation in two. The second function was the execution of *national strategy*: the mobilization of the political, economic, diplomatic, and psychological as well as military resources of the nation to achieve this war aim. By 1864 Union national strategy had become policy as well; a week before he sent this telegram to Grant, Lincoln had been renominated for president on a platform pledging "unconditional surrender" of the Confederacy *and* a constitutional amendment to abolish slavery.[1]

Neither of these objectives, however, could be achieved without winning the war. As commander in chief, Lincoln found it necessary to take an active part in formulating *military strategy*. He had long since concluded that the war could not be won merely by capturing Southern real estate including key cities—which the Union army and navy had been doing very successfully for more than two years—but by destroying the Confederate armies that kept the rebellion alive. When the Army of Northern Virginia had marched north in June 1863 on the campaign that would climax at Gettysburg, Union commander Joseph Hooker proposed to attack the weakened defenses of Richmond instead of confronting Lee. Lincoln rejected this idea. "Lee's Army, and not Richmond, is your true objective point," the President told Hooker.[2] Three months later, as the two armies maneuvered and skirmished over the devastated land between Washington and Richmond, Lincoln declared that "to attempt to fight the enemy back to his intrenchments in Richmond . . . is an idea I have been trying to repudiate for quite a year. . . . I have constantly desired the Army of the Potomac, to make Lee's army, and not Richmond, it's objective point. If our army can not fall upon the enemy and hurt him where he is, it is plain to me it can gain nothing by attempting to follow him over a succession of intrenched lines into a fortified city."[3]

Lincoln therefore approved heartily of Grant's decision to slice Lee's supply line at Petersburg rather than to continue attacking the Confederate defenses at Cold Harbor. He expected Grant's movement to force Lee into the open for the showdown battle to destroy the Confederacy's premier army that Lincoln had sought for two years. "You will succeed," Lincoln optimistically told Grant in the June 15 telegram.[4] But once again, Lincoln's—and Grant's—subordinates failed the commander in chief and general in chief. They failed to press home the attack at Petersburg on June 15—the very day of Lincoln's telegram—giving Lee time to rush reinforcements to its defense. It was one more example of how the commander in chief's sound military strategy was undermined by the failures of his field commanders. Grant was compelled to settle down for a siege that would last more than nine months, ending on April 2, 1865, when Lee's Army of Northern Virginia abandoned Petersburg. By that time, General Sherman's march through Georgia and into South Carolina coupled with General Thomas's destruction of the Army of Tennessee had shattered the Confederacy, and Lee surrendered to Grant at Appomattox Court House on April 9, 1865, ending the war.

NOTES

1. Edward McPherson, *The Political History of the United States during the Great Rebellion*, 2nd ed. (Washington D.C.: Philp and Solomons, 1865), 406-407.

2. Abraham Lincoln to Joseph Hooker, June 10, 1863, *The Collected Works of Abraham Lincoln*, ed. Roy P. Basler, 9 vols. (New Brunswick, NJ: Rutgers University Press, 1953-55), 6: 257.

3. Abraham Lincoln to Henry W. Halleck, September 19, 1863, *Collected Works*, 6: 467.

4. Abraham Lincoln to Ulysses S. Grant, June 15, 1864, The Gilder Lehrman Collection, on deposit at the New-York Historical Society (GLC01572); also printed in *Collected Works*, 7: 393.

[*TRANSCRIPT*]

Lincoln to Ulysses S. Grant, June 15, 1864.

Washington, June 15, 1864

Lieu^t. Gen. Grant
    Head Q^{rs}. A.P.

Have just read your despatch of 1 p.m. yesterday. I begin to see it. You will succeed. God bless you all.

A.Lincoln

A telegram from Abraham Lincoln to Ulysses S. Grant, June 15, 1864. (GLC01572)

[9]

Lincoln and the Passage of the Thirteenth Amendment, 1865

==

BY ALLEN C. GUELZO*

THOSE WHO KNEW Mr. Lincoln best," wrote Illinois Congressman Isaac Arnold, "knew that he looked, confidently, to the ultimate extinction of slavery" and used "every means which his prudent and scrupulous mind recognized as right and proper, to hasten its ultimate overthrow."[1] This was, however, no easy aspiration for Abraham Lincoln, even as president. Slavery was protected from the touch of presidents (and the rest of the federal government) by state law, and the best Lincoln could have hoped to accomplish when he became president in 1861 was to prevent slavery's growth beyond the fifteen Southern states where it was then legal.

The attempted secession, after Lincoln's election, of eleven of those states to form the Confederacy changed that situation, and allowed Lincoln to move against slavery as an object of war. Flexing his "war powers" as the "Commander in Chief of the Army and Navy of the United States," Lincoln issued an Emancipation Proclamation on January 1, 1863, which declared all of the slaves held in the rebel states "thenceforward, and forever, free."

But even as commander in chief, Lincoln's hands were not entirely free to strike slavery down. For one thing, his presidential "war powers" only gave him authority to reach slaves in rebel-held territory—not the four border states of Missouri, Delaware, Kentucky, and Maryland, which remained loyal to the Union but where slavery remained legal, nor the portions of the rebel states which had been reconquered by federal forces by January 1863. Also, the Emancipation Proclamation freed *slaves*—it did

*ALLEN C. GUELZO *is Henry R. Luce Professor of the Civil War Era and Director of the Civil War Era Studies Program at Gettysburg College. He won the Lincoln Prize in 2000 for* Abraham Lincoln: Redeemer President *(1999) and in 2005 for* Lincoln's Emancipation Proclamation: The End of Slavery in America *(2004).*

In this detail from "Emancipation," Thomas Nast depicts African Americans' hopes inspired by the Emancipation Proclamation. This image was republished in 1865 when the Thirteenth Amendment was passed. (Broadside published by S. Bott, Philadelphia, Pa., c. 1865. Library of Congress Prints and Photographs Division.)

not end *slavery* as a legal institution. Above all, Lincoln worried about the federal courts, which were reluctant to recognize any such presidential war powers.

The only way to make emancipation stick, and to cleanse the nation entirely from slavery, was to amend the Constitution. There was, however, little hope of persuading Congress to adopt such an amendment, or to expect the states to ratify it, during the first two years of the war. The Emancipation Proclamation stimulated a political backlash among white Northerners that cost Republicans thirty-one seats in Congress, and led to race riots in northern cities in the summer of 1863. That December, when Congress assembled, James Ashley of Ohio introduced a resolution in the House of Representatives to amend the Constitution by abolishing slavery, followed by a similar resolution in the Senate. The Senate gave the amendment a solid 38-to-6 approval in April 1864. But after six months of debate, the proposed amendment won only 93 votes in the House, well short of the two-thirds majority required by the Constitution for amendments.[2]

However, despite fears to the contrary, in the fall of 1864, Lincoln won a resounding re-election, and with that momentum behind him, he endorsed the proposed amendment as the only way to "meet and cover all cavils" about the abolition of slavery.[3] In his December 1864 annual message to Congress (reprinted here), he called for "reconsideration and passage" of James Ashley's "proposed amendment of the Constitution, abolishing slavery throughout the United States."[4] And when Ashley moved reconsideration on January 6, 1865, Lincoln went to work, dangling rewards and twisting congressional arms, until on January 31, the reconsideration squeaked through the House by seven votes.[5]

The amendment resolution was signed by the Speaker of the House—Indiana representative (and future vice-president) Schuyler Colfax—and by Lincoln's vice president, Hannibal Hamlin of Maine, as presiding officer of the Senate, with certification by John W. Forney (whose Washington newspaper, the *Daily Morning Chronicle*, was ardently pro-Lincoln) as secretary of the Senate and by Edward McPherson (whose family farm had been fought over during the battle of Gettysburg) for the House. And although the amendment process does not require a presidential signature, Lincoln nevertheless signed his name to the resolution the next day, writing out in full (as he rarely did), *Abraham Lincoln*.

The text of the amendment—the thirteenth in the sequence of constitutional amendments—is simplicity at its simplest. "Neither slavery nor involuntary servitude, except as punishment for crime whereof the party shall have been duly convicted, shall exist within the United States, or any place subject to their jurisdiction." That evening, after signing the resolution, Lincoln described the passage of the Thirteenth Amendment as an "occasion . . . of congratulation to the country and to the whole world." For all those who feared "whether the [Emancipation] proclamation was legally valid," the Thirteenth Amendment provided "a King's cure for all the evils," as though slavery were a kind of scrofula, which only the touch of an ultimate authority could make disappear.[6] The amendment would be formally ratified on December 6, 1865—a ratification that Lincoln, sadly, would not live to see.

NOTES

1. Isaac Arnold, *The History of Abraham Lincoln and the Overthrow of Slavery* (Chicago: Clarke & Co., 1866), 218.

2. Henry Wilson, *History of the Anti-Slavery Measures of the Thirty-Seventh and Thirty-Eighth United-States Congresses, 1861-64* (Boston: Walker, Wise & Co., 1864), 247, 265, 271.

3. Abraham Lincoln, Reply to committee notifying Lincoln of his renomination, June 9, 1864, *Collected Works of Abraham Lincoln*, ed. Roy P. Basler, 9 vols. (New Brunswick, NJ: Rutgers University Press, 1953-55), 7: 380.

4. Abraham Lincoln, Fragment of last annual message to Congress concerning the Thirteenth Amendment, December 6, 1864, The Gilder Lehrman Collection, on deposit at the New-York Historical Society (GLC08094).

5. Michael Vorenberg, *Final Freedom: The Civil War, the Abolition of Slavery, and the Thirteenth Amendment* (Cambridge and New York: Cambridge University Press, 2001), 253.

6. Abraham Lincoln, Response to a Serenade, February 1, 1865, *Collected Works*, 8: 254.

[T R A N S C R I P T]

A fragment of Lincoln's notes for his annual message to Congress concerning the Thirteenth Amendment, December 6, 1864.

At the last session of Congress a proposed amendment of the Constitution abolishing slavery throughout the United States, passed the Senate, but failed for lack of the requisite two thirds vote in the House of Representatives. Although the present is the same Congress, and nearly the same members, and without questioning the wisdom or patriotism of those who stood in opposition, I venture to recommend the reconsideration and passage of the measure at the present session.

Notes by Abraham Lincoln for his last annual message to Congress, December 6, 1864. (GLC08094)

[*TRANSCRIPT*]

The Thirteenth Amendment Resolution, February 1, 1865.

Thirty-Eighth Congress

of the United States of America, at the second session, begun and held at the City of Washington on Monday the fifth day of December one thousand eight hundred and sixty-four.

A Resolution

submitting to the legislatures of the several states a proposition to amend the Constitution of the United States.

Resolved by the Senate and House of Representatives of the United States of America in Congress assembled, two-thirds of both Houses concurring. That the following article be proposed to the legislatures of the several states as an amendment to the Constitution of the United States which, when ratified by three-fourths of said legislatures shall be valid to all intents and purposes, as a part of the said Constitution, namely:

Article XIII.

Sec. 1. Neither slavery nor involuntary servitude, except as a punishment for crime whereof the party shall have been duly convicted, shall exist within the United States, or any place subject to their jurisdiction.
Sec. 2. Congress shall have power to enforce this article by appropriate legislation.

I certify that this Resolution	Schuyler Colfax	Speaker of the House of Representatives
originated in the Senate	H. Hamlin.	Vice-President of the United States and
J.W. Forney, Secretary		President of the Senate,

Attest E McPherson
Clerk of the House of Representatives

Approved February 1. A.D. 1865.   Abraham Lincoln

[Signatures appear on page 68.]

The Thirteenth Amendment, passed by the Senate in April 1864 and the House of Representatives on January 31, 1865, was signed by Abraham Lincoln on February 1, 1865. (GLC00263)

[Signatures from the bottom of the document printed on page 67.]

In the Senate April 8. 1864

1. S. C. Pomeroy	11. Lyman Trumbull			
2. W. T. Willey	12. L. F. S. Foster			
3. H. S. Lane	13. Solomon Foot	21. J. Collamer	28. Edgar Cowan	36. Timy. O Howe
4. L. M. Morrill	14. Jn C. Ten Eyck	22. B. F. Wade	29. John P. Hale	37. James W. Grimes
5. J. W. Nesmith	15. James Dixon		30. B. Gratz Brown	
6. J. R. Doolittle	16. J. H. Lane	23. J. B. Henderson	31. J. M. Howard	
7. Reverdy Johnson	17. Alex. Ramsey	24. Ira Harris	32. H. B. Anthony	
8. P. C. Van Winkle	18. Jas. Harlan	25. Wm Sprague	33. John Conness	
9. M. S. Wilkinson	19. E. D Morgan	26. Charles Sumner	34. Henry Wilson	
10. Z. Chandler	20. Daniel Clark	27. L. M. Morrill	35. John Sherman	

In the House of Representatives January 31. 1865

Isaac N. Arnold	Schuyler Colfax	Henry G. Worthington	Thaddeus Stevens	Alex. H. Rice
J. F. Driggs	Henry C. Deming	E. R. Eckley	Justin S. Morrill	Amasa Cobb
Luc. Anderson	Fredck E. Woodbridge	Wm. Higby	N. B. Smithers	J. M. Broomall
J. M. Marvin	Cornelius Cole	D. W. Gooch	Theodore M. Pomeroy	C. T. Hulburd N.Y.
J. A. Garfield	John D. Baldwin	Portus Baxter	W. B. Washburn	R. B. Van Valkenburg
Oakes Ames Mas.	Wm. B. Allison	F. W. Kellogg	A. W. Hubbard	Francis Thomas
H. Price	E Dumont	Rufus P. Spalding	Chas. O'Neill	J.W. Patterson N. H.
E. C. Ingersoll	Geo. S. Boutwell	Jesse O. Norton	H. W. Tracy	John A. Kasson
H. L. Dawes	S. Hooper	John B. Steele	Jno. W. Longyear	E. C. Washburne Ill.
John H. Rice	M. Russell Thayer	Thomas D. Eliot	James T. Hale	Sidney Perham
F. C. Beaman	A. Myers Pa.	Wm. D. Kelley	D. Morris N.Y.	Wm. G. Brown W. Va
Sempronius H. Boyd	J. M Ashley	D. C. Littlejohn	John H. Hubbard	J. F. Farnsworth
James F. Wilson	T. A. Jenckes	Nathan F. Dixon R. I.	A. C. Wilder Kan.	S. F. Miller N.Y.
F. Clarke	I. C. Sloan	Orlando S. Kellogg	Chas. Upson	Henry T. Blow
Jno R. McBride	J. W. McClurg Mo.	Leonard Myers	John A. Griswold	Thos. T. Davis N. Y.
James E. English	Thom Williams Pa.	Edwin H. Webster	Aug. C. Baldwin	Wm. Windom
Augustus Frank	Ignatius Donnelly	A. McAllister	Godlove S. Orth	W. H. Randall
Samuel Knox	Fred A Pike	Giles W. Hotchkiss	E. H. Rollins	K. V. Whaley
John B Alley Ma	Benjn. F. Loan Mo.	T. B. Shannon	M. F. Odell	Anson Herrick N.Y.
Augustus Brandegee	Geo. H. Yeaman	J. G. Blaine	G. W. Scofield	A. H. Coffroth
	J. B. Grinnell Iowa	W. A. Hutchins	Ezra Wheeler	Jacob B. Blair
	G. Clay Smith	J. K. Moorhead Pa.	H. A. Nelson	H. Winter Davis
		Austin A. King	Joseph Baily	Rbt C. Schenck

[10]

Lincoln's Second Inaugural Address

BY RONALD C. WHITE, JR.*

O N M A R C H 4, 1865, the day of his second inauguration, Abraham Lincoln was looking to the future. He was the first president to be inaugurated for a second term in thirty-two years, in a nation only seventy-six years old, and gamblers in the street were betting that he would be inaugurated for a third term in 1869. Although Lincoln would make no predictions about it, all signs indicated that the Civil War, a war that cost as many American lives as all of our other wars put together, was coming to an end.

The address that Lincoln delivered on a cold, blustery day caught everyone by surprise. The audience was prepared to cheer rhetoric praising the North and denigrating the South. Lincoln offered neither. Surely, they thought, the President would offer specific plans for what was being called "reconstruction" after the war. He did not. Instead, Lincoln spoke to the future, when everyone around him was clinging fiercely to the past. His goal was to begin the healing that would lead to reconciliation.

Lincoln's Second Inaugural, at 701 words, remains the second shortest inaugural address in American history.[1] In the first two paragraphs Lincoln writes almost as a chronicler standing outside the events. Here, he uses "I" and "myself," but offers no personal pronouns in the rest of the address. He directs all the attention away from himself. The word "war" dominates the second paragraph. But when Lincoln, speaking slowly and sadly, intoned, "And the war came," he was acknowledging that, despite his plans and those of his generals, this war, with its 620,000 dead, had assumed an inexorable momentum.

By introducing the Bible in the third paragraph, Lincoln entered new territory. In the previous eighteen inaugural addresses, only John Quincy Adams had quoted

* RONALD C. WHITE, JR., *is the author of* A. Lincoln: A Biography *(2009) and* Lincoln's Greatest Speech: The Second Inaugural *(2002). He is Visiting Professor of History at the University of California, Los Angeles, and a Fellow at the Huntington Library.*

THE INAUGURAL ADDRESS

OF PRESIDENT

ABRAHAM LINCOLN,

DELIVERED AT THE NATIONAL CAPITOL,

MARCH 4th, 1865.

Fellow Countrymen:

At this second appearing to take the oath of the Presidential Office, there is less occasion for an extended address than there was at the first. Then a statement somewhat in detail of a course to be pursued seemed very fitting and proper. Now, at the expiration of four years, during which public declarations have been constantly called forth on every point and phase of the great contest which still absorbs the attention and engrosses the energies of the nation, little that is new could be presented.

The progress of our arms—upon which all else chiefly depends—is as well known to the public as to myself; and it is, I trust, reasonably satisfactory and encouraging to all. With high hope for the future, no prediction in regard to it is ventured.

On the occasion corresponding to this four years ago, all thoughts were anxiously directed to an impending civil war. All dreaded it; all sought to avoid it. While the inaugural address was being delivered from this place, devoted altogether to saving the Union without war, insurgent agents were in the city seeking to destroy it without war—seeking to dissolve the Union and divide the effects by negotiation.

Both parties deprecated war; but one of them would make war rather than let the nation survive, and the other would accept war rather than let it perish, and the war came.

One-eighth of the whole population were colored slaves, not distributed generally over the Union, but localized in the Southern part of it. These slaves constituted a peculiar and powerful interest. All knew that this interest was somehow the cause of the war. To strengthen, perpetuate and extend this interest was the object for which the insurgents would rend the Union by war, while the Government claimed no right to do more than to restrict the territorial enlargement of it.

Neither party expected for the war the magnitude or the duration which it has already attained. Neither anticipated that the cause of the conflict might cease, even before the conflict itself should cease. Each looked for an easier triumph and a result less fundamental and astounding.

Both read the same Bible, and pray to the same God, and each invokes His aid against the other. It may seem strange that any men should dare to ask a just God's assistance in wringing their bread from the sweat of other men's faces; but let us judge not, that we be not judged. The prayers of both should not be answered. That of neither has been answered fully. The Almighty has His own purposes. Woe unto the world because of offences, for it must needs be that offences come; but woe to that man by whom the offence cometh. If we shall suppose that American Slavery is one of these offences—which, in the providence of God, must needs come, but which, having continued through His appointed time, He now wills to remove, and that He gives to both North and South this terrible war as the woe due to those by whom the offence came—shall we discern there is any departure from those Divine attributes which the believers in a living God always ascribe to Him? Fondly do we hope, fervently do we pray, that this mighty scourge of war may speedily pass away. Yet, if God wills that it continue until all the wealth piled by the bondman's two hundred and fifty years of unrequited toil shall be sunk, and until every drop of blood drawn with the lash shall be paid by another drawn with the sword, as was said three thousand years ago, so still it must be said that the judgments of the Lord are true and righteous altogether.

With malice toward none, with charity for all, with firmness in the right, as God gives us to see the right, let us strive on to finish the work we are in, to bind up the nation's wound, to care for him who shall have borne the battle, and for his widow and orphans; to do all which may achieve and cherish a just and a lasting peace among ourselves and with all nations.

Abraham Lincoln's Second Inaugural Address, published as a broadside for distribution. (GLC06044)

President Lincoln delivers his Second Inaugural Address on the steps of the Capitol, March 4, 1865. (Library of Congress Prints and Photographs Division)

from the Bible. From this paragraph to the end of the address, Lincoln quotes the Bible four times, names God fourteen times, and mentions prayer three times, giving this address a distinctively spiritual tone and cadence. Some contemporary commentators called it "Lincoln's Sermon on the Mount."

As the address builds toward its final paragraph, Lincoln makes an unexpected political and rhetorical move. He invokes the Gospel of Matthew to convince the nation that the war was the judgment of God for the offense of slavery. His depiction of American slavery conveys his understanding that the whole nation, not the South alone, was responsible for it. His phrase "until every drop of blood drawn with the lash, shall be paid by another drawn with the sword" is far more evocative than the reasoned language of Lincoln the lawyer referencing the Constitution in his First Inaugural Address.

In the final paragraph, which begins "With malice toward none; with charity for all," Lincoln asks his fellow Americans to look forward to a new era, armed not with hostility but with forgiveness. He concludes his address with a coda of healing:

> to bind up. . .
>   to care for. . .
>   to do all which may achieve and cherish a just,
>   and a lasting peace.

The young Charles Francis Adams, Jr., was in the crowd that day. Adams counted two presidents, John Adams and John Quincy Adams, in his lineage. His father, Charles Francis Adams, had served as Minister to England since 1861. Adams wrote his father in London on Tuesday, March 7, offering his appraisal of the speech: "That rail-splitting lawyer is one of the wonders of the day. Once at Gettysburg and now again on a greater occasion he has shown a capacity for rising to the demands of the hour." Adams concluded, "This inaugural strikes me in its grand simplicity and directness as being for all time the historical keynote of this war."[2]

With Lincoln's death, just forty-one days after his inauguration, the words of this address took on a new meaning. Carved into the Indiana limestone of the Lincoln Memorial in 1922, the Second Inaugural remains less well known than the Gettysburg Address, but Lincoln thought it his finest speech. Responding to words of congratulations from New York Republican Thurlow Weed, Lincoln revealed his estimation of the speech and modestly predicted that it would endure, "perhaps better than anything I have produced."[3]

NOTES

1. George Washington's second inaugural address, at 135 words, was simply an acknowledgement of his election.

2. Charles Francis Adams Jr. to Charles Francis Adams Sr., March 7, 1865, *A Cycle of Adams Letters, 1861-1865*, ed. Worthington Chauncey Fort (Boston and New York: Houghton Mifflin, 1920), 257-58.

3. Abraham Lincoln to Thurlow Weed, March 15, 1865, in *The Collected Works of Abraham Lincoln*, ed. Roy P. Basler, 9 vols. (New Brunswick, NJ: Rutgers University Press, 1953-55), 8: 356.

[11]

"Kin": Frederick Douglass and Abraham Lincoln

——

BY DAVID W. BLIGHT*

FREDERICK DOUGLASS attended President Abraham Lincoln's second inauguration on March 4, 1865. Standing in the crowd, Douglass heard Lincoln declare slavery the "cause" and emancipation the "result" of the Civil War. Over the crisp air he heard Lincoln's determination that to win the war "every drop of blood drawn with the lash shall be paid by another drawn with the sword."[1] Four years earlier, and many times in between, Douglass had dreamed of writing that speech for Lincoln. That the President himself wrote it in those tragic days of spring 1865 is a testament to the power of events, to Lincoln's own moral fiber, and to the political and rhetorical bond he shared with Douglass.

Douglass attended the inaugural reception that evening at the Executive Mansion. At first denied entrance by two policemen, Douglass was admitted only when the President himself was notified. Weary of a lifetime of such racial rejections, Douglass was immediately set at ease by Lincoln's cordial greeting: "Here comes my friend Douglass." Lincoln asked Douglass what he thought of the day's speech. Douglass demurred, urging the President to attend to his host of visitors. But Lincoln insisted, telling his black guest: "There is no man in the country whose opinion I value more than yours." "Mr. Lincoln," replied the former slave, "that was a sacred effort."[2] We can only guess at the thrill in Douglass's heart, knowing that the cause he had so long pleaded—a sanctioned war to destroy slavery and potentially to reinvent the American republic around the principle of racial equality—might now come to fruition. He could fairly entertain the

* DAVID W. BLIGHT *is Class of '54 Professor of American History at Yale University and Director of the Gilder Lehrman Center for the Study of Slavery, Resistance, and Abolition. He received the Frederick Douglass Book Prize in 2001 and the Lincoln Prize in 2002 for* Race and Reunion: The Civil War in American Memory *(2001).*

[73]

belief that he and Lincoln, the slaves and the nation, were walking that night into a new history.

But nothing during the early months of Reconstruction came easily, especially in the wake of Lincoln's assassination at the dawn of peace. In her grief, and with the assistance of her personal aide, Elizabeth Keckley, Mary Todd Lincoln sent mementos to special people. Among the recipients of some of the President's canes were the black abolitionist Henry Highland Garnet and a White House servant, William Slade. But to Douglass Mrs. Lincoln sent the President's "favorite walking staff" (on display today at Cedar Hill, Douglass's home in Washington, D.C.). In his remarkable letter of reply, reproduced here, Douglass assured the First Lady that he would forever possess the cane as an "object of sacred interest," not only for himself, but because of Mr. Lincoln's "humane interest in the welfare of my whole race."[3] In this expression of gratitude, Douglass evoked the enduring symbolic bond between the sixteenth President and many African Americans.

Douglass's relationship with Lincoln had not always been so warm. Indeed, Douglass's attitude toward Lincoln moved from cautious support in 1860 to outrage in 1861-62, and eventually to respect and admiration in 1863-65. At the outset of the war Douglass wanted precisely what Lincoln did not want: a "remorseless revolutionary struggle" that would make black freedom indispensable to saving the Union.[4] In September 1861, Douglass denounced Lincoln's revocation of General John C. Fremont's unauthorized emancipation order in Missouri. In 1862-63 he was offended by the administration's plans for colonization of the freed people. Indeed, nothing disappointed Douglass as much as the President's August 1862 meeting with a black delegation at the White House, when Lincoln told his guests that "we [the two races] should be separated" and that the only hope for equality rested in their emigration to a new land.[5] Douglass reprinted Lincoln's remarks in his newspaper and penned his harshest criticism ever of the President, calling him an "itinerant colonization lecturer" and a "genuine representative of American prejudice."[6]

But much changed in Douglass's estimation of Lincoln with the advent of the Emancipation Proclamation and the policy of recruiting black soldiers in 1863. As the war expanded in scale and purpose, Lincoln and Douglass began to move toward a shared vision of its meaning. On August 10, 1863, Douglass visited Washington, D.C., for the first time and met with Lincoln for a frank discussion of discrimination practiced against black troops. Lincoln said he understood the anguish over unequal pay for black men, but considered it a "necessary concession" in order to achieve the larger aim of getting blacks into uniform. Although they did not agree on all issues,

Frederick Douglass actively supported the recruitment of African Americans into the Union army, once the Emancipation Proclamation allowed them to enlist. Eventually more than 180,000 black soldiers served. (Photograph of Co. E, 4th U.S. Colored Infantry at Fort Lincoln, 1865. Courtesy Library of Congress Prints and Photographs Division.)

Douglass came away from this meeting impressed with Lincoln's forthrightness and respectful of the President's political skills. Douglass relished opportunities to tell of his first meeting with Lincoln. "I felt big there," he told a lecture audience, describing how secretaries admitted him to Lincoln's office ahead of a long line of office-seekers. Disarmed, even awed, by Lincoln's directness, Douglass remembered that the President looked him in the eye and said: "Remember this . . . remember that Milliken's Bend, Port Hudson, and Fort Wagner are recent events; and . . . were necessary to prepare the way for this very proclamation of mine."[7] For the first time, Douglass expressed a personal identification with Lincoln. The "rebirth" of the nation about which Lincoln spoke so famously at Gettysburg in November 1863 had long been Douglass's favorite metaphor as well.

By the end of 1863, Lincoln and Douglass spoke from virtually the same script, one of them with the elegance and restraint of a statesman, and the other the fiery tones of a prophet. In his Annual Message of December 8, 1863, Lincoln declared that "the policy of emancipation . . . gave to the future a new aspect." The nation was engaged in a "new reckoning" in which it might become "the home of freedom disentralled, regenerated, enlarged."[8] Lincoln's language makes a striking comparison to a speech Douglass delivered many time across the North in the winter of 1863-64. In "The Mission of the War" Douglass declared that however long the "shadow of death" cast over the land, Americans should not forget the moral "grandeur" of the struggle. "It is the manifest destiny of this war," he announced, "to unify and reorganized the institutions of the country," and thereby give the scale of death its "sacred significance."

"The mission of this war," Douglass concluded, "is National regeneration."[9] Together, Lincoln and Douglass had provided the subjunctive and declarative voices of the Second American Revolution—and by the last year of the war, they were nearly one and the same.

In the summer of 1864, with the war at a bloody stalemate in Virginia, Lincoln's reelection was in jeopardy and Douglass's support of him temporarily waned. He briefly considered supporting John C. Fremont's candidacy to unseat Lincoln in the Republican Party. But in August Lincoln invited Douglass to the White House for their extraordinary second meeting. The President was under heavy pressure from all sides: Copperheads condemned him for pursuing an abolitionist war, while abolitionists sought to replace him with the more radical Fremont. Lincoln was worried that the war might end without complete victory and the end of slavery, so he sought Douglass's advice. Lincoln had drafted a letter, denying that he was standing in the way of peace and declaring that he could not sustain a war to destroy slavery if Congress did not will it. Douglass urged Lincoln not to publish the letter and ultimately, because of events and perhaps Douglass's advice, he never did.

Even more importantly, Lincoln asked Douglass to lead a scheme reminiscent of John Brown and Harpers Ferry. Concerned that if he were not reelected, the Democrats would pursue a negotiated, proslavery peace, Lincoln, according to Douglass, wanted "to get more of the slaves within our lines." Douglass went North and organized some twenty-five agents who were willing to work at the front. In a letter to Lincoln on August 29, 1864, Douglass outlined his plan for a "band of scouts" channeling slaves northward. Douglass was not convinced that this plan was fully "practicable," but he was ready to serve.[10] Because military fortunes shifted dramatically with the fall of Atlanta, this government-sponsored underground railroad never materialized. But how remarkable this episode must have been to both Douglass and Lincoln as they realized they were working together now to accomplish the very "revolution" that had separated them ideologically in 1861. Garry Wills has argued that Lincoln performed a "verbal coup" that "revolutionized the revolution" at Gettysburg.[11] By 1864, that performance reflected a shared vision of the meaning of the war. Ideologically, Douglass had become Lincoln's alter ego, his stalking horse and minister of propaganda, the intellectual godfather of the Gettysburg Address and the Second Inaugural.

When news of Lincoln's assassination reached Rochester on April 15, 1865, Douglass had just returned from a lecture tour on which he witnessed great joy at the war's ending. He shared the shock of fellow Northerners as a springtime of relief turned overnight into horror and mourning. A throng of Rochester citizens gathered at City Hall, as Douglass remembered, "not knowing what to do in the agony of the hour." Called upon to speak, Douglass described himself as "stunned and overwhelmed." "I had . . . made many speeches there [Rochester] which had touched the hearts of my hearers," he recalled, "but never to this day was I brought into such close accord with them. We shared in common a terrible calamity, and this touch of nature made us more than countrymen, it made us Kin."[12]

Douglass would later write brilliantly and honestly about the necessity and the struggle of African Americans to sustain their sense of kinship with white Americans and with Abraham Lincoln. But history, with Douglass and Lincoln indispensably bound, had forged the possibility of such a national kinship—itself a brave American dream.

NOTES

1. Abraham Lincoln, Second Inaugural Address, March 4, 1865, *The Collected Works of Abraham Lincoln*, ed. Roy P. Basler, 9 vols. (New Brunswick, NJ: Rutgers University Press, 1953-55), 8: 333.

2. Frederick Douglass, *The Life and Times of Frederick Douglass: From 1817-1882*, ed. John Lobb (London: Christian Age Office, 1882), 321.

3. Frederick Douglass to Mary Todd Lincoln, August 17, 1865, The Gilder Lehrman Collection, on deposit at the New-York Historical Society (GLC02474); also published in *The Life and Writings of Frederick Douglass*, ed. Philip S. Foner, 5 vols. (New York: International Publishers, 1975), 4: 174.

4. Abraham Lincoln, Annual message to Congress, December 3, 1861, *Collected Works*, 5: 49.

5. Abraham Lincoln, Address on colonization to a deputation of negroes, August 14, 1862, *Collected Works*, 5: 371.

6. Frederick Douglass, "The President and His Speeches," September 1862, *Douglass' Monthly* in *The Life and Writings of Frederick Douglass*, 3: 267-268.

7. Frederick Douglass, "Our Work Is Not Done," December 3-4, 1863, *The Life and Writings of Frederick Douglass*, 3: 383-385.

8. Abraham Lincoln, Annual message to Congress, December 8, 1863, *Collected Works*, 7: 49-53.

9. Frederick Douglass, "The Mission of the War," February 13, 1864, *The Life and Writings of Frederick Douglass*, 3: 397-401.

10. Frederick Douglass to Abraham Lincoln, August 29, 1864, *The Life and Writings of Frederick Douglass*, 3: 405

11. Gary Wills, *Lincoln at Gettysburg: The Words That Remade America* (New York: Simon & Schuster, 1992), 21.

12. *The Life and Times of Frederick Douglass: From 1817-1882*, 326.

Frederick Douglass, c. 1870 (GLC06198) and Mary Todd Lincoln in mourning, c. 1869 (Abraham Lincoln Presidential Library and Museum).

⸢ *TRANSCRIPT* ⸣

Frederick Douglass to Mary Todd Lincoln, August 17, 1865.

Rochester. N.Y. August 17. 1865.

Mrs Abraham Lincoln:

Dear Madam: Allow me to thank you, as I certainly do thank you most sincerely for your thoughtful kindness in making me the owner of a Cane—which was formerly the property and the favorite walking staff of your late lamented husband the honored and venerated President of the United States.

I assure you, that this inestimable memmento of his Excellency will be retained in my possession while I live—an object of sacred interest—a token not merely of the kind Consideration in which I have reason to know that the President was pleased to hold me personally, but ~~of~~ as an indication of ~~the~~ his humane ~~consideration~~ interest [in the] welfare of my whole race.

With every proper sentiment of Respect and Esteem
I am, Dear Madam, your Obe^dt Servt.
Frederick Douglass.

Rochester. N.Y. August 17. 1865.

Mrs Abraham Lincoln:

Dear Madam: Allow me to thank
you, as I certainly do thank you most sincerely for
your thoughtful kindness in making me the owner
of a Cane - which was formerly the property and the
favorite walking Staff of your late lamented husband the
honored and venerated President of the United States.

I assure you, that this inestimable memento of his
Excellency will be retained in my possession while I live
- an object of Sacred interest - a token not merely of
the kind Consideration in which I have reason to know
that, the President was pleased to hold me personally, but
as an indication of his humane ~~dedication~~ interest
welfare of my whole race.

With every proper sentiment of Respect and Esteem
I am, Dear Madam, your Obo.dt Servt
Frederick Douglass.

A letter from Frederick Douglass to Mary Todd Lincoln, August 17, 1865. (GLC02474)

Abraham Lincoln: A Timeline

—

1809	February 12	Born in a one-room log cabin near Hodgenville, Ky., to Thomas and Nancy Hanks Lincoln.
1816	December	Lincoln's family moves to Spencer County, Ind.
1818	October 5	Lincoln's mother, Nancy Hanks Lincoln, dies.
1819	December 2	Lincoln's father marries Sarah Bush Johnston, a widow with three children.
1828	Spring	Takes a flatboat of farm produce to New Orleans, where he is reported to have observed a slave auction.
1830	March	Lincoln's family moves near Decatur, Ill.
1831	April-July	Makes a second flatboat trip to New Orleans.
	July	Moves to New Salem, Ill., where he works as a store clerk.
1832	April 7	Elected captain of his rifle company during the Black Hawk War.
	Summer	In his first election campaign, runs for Illinois General Assembly and loses.
1833		Appointed postmaster of New Salem and deputy county surveyor.
1834	July	Begins to study law on his own.
	August 4	Elected to the Illinois General Assembly as a Whig.
1836	August 1	Reelected to the Illinois General Assembly (second term).
	September 9	Receives his law license.
1837	April 15	Moves to Springfield, Ill., and begins practicing law.
1838	August 6	Reelected to the Illinois General Assembly (third term).
1840	August 3	Reelected to the Illinois General Assembly (fourth and final term).
1842	November 4	Marries Mary Todd.
1843	August 1	b. Robert Todd Lincoln, Abraham and Mary Todd Lincoln's first son.
1846	March 10	b. Edward Baker Lincoln, the Lincolns' second son.
	August 3	Elected to the U.S. House of Representatives.
1847	December 22	Presents his "Spot Resolutions" against the Mexican War in U.S. House of Representatives.
1849	May 22	Receives U.S. Patent No. 6,469 for a device to raise boats over shoals.
1850	February 1	d. Eddie Lincoln, the Lincolns' second son.
	December 21	b. William Wallace (Willie) Lincoln, the Lincolns' third son.
1853	April 4	b. Thomas (Tad) Lincoln, the Lincolns' fourth son.
1854	October 16	Delivers pivotal speech in Peoria, Ill., against Kansas-Nebraska Act.

1855	February	Loses first campaign for U.S. Senate.
1856		Helps organize Illinois Republican party.
	June 19	Receives 110 votes for vice president at Republican National Convention.
1857	June 26	Denounces U.S. Supreme Court *Dred Scott* decision.
1858	June 16	Receives Republican nomination for U. S. Senate and delivers "House Divided" speech; campaign is unsuccessful.
	Aug.-Oct.	Engages in seven debates with Stephen Douglas for Senate seat.
1860	February 27	Gives Cooper Union address in New York.
	May 18	Wins Republican Party nomination for President.
	November 6	Elected 16th President of the United States.
	December 20	South Carolina secedes from the Union.
1861	March 4	Delivers First Inaugural Address.
	April 12	Fort Sumter in Charleston, S.C., is attacked and surrenders.
	August 6	First Confiscation Act, freeing slaves used by Confederates in the war.
1862	February 20	*d.* Willie Lincoln, age eleven.
	April 16	Signs act abolishing slavery in the District of Columbia.
	July 17	Second Confiscation Act extends power of Union military to free Southern slaves.
	July 22	Submits draft of Emancipation Proclamation to the Cabinet.
	August 14	Delivers "Address on Colonization to a Deputation of Free Blacks."
	September 22	Issues Preliminary Emancipation Proclamation.
1863	January 1	Emancipation Proclamation goes into effect.
	March 3	Signs bill authorizing military conscription.
	November 19	Delivers Gettysburg Address.
1864	March 10	Appoints Ulysses S. Grant general in chief of U.S. Army.
	June 8	Renominated as Republicans' presidential candidate.
	August 19	Meets with Frederick Douglass at White House for second time.
	November 8	Reelected President.
	December 20	Sherman captures Savannah, Ga., completing "march to the sea."
1865	February 1	Signs the Thirteenth Amendment, abolishing slavery.
	March 4	Delivers Second Inaugural Address.
	April 9	Lee surrenders to Grant at Appomattox Court House, Va.
	April 11	Makes his last public speech, focusing on reconstruction.
	April 14	Shot by John Wilkes Booth at Ford's Theatre in Washington, D.C.
	April 15	Dies at 7:22 am.
	May 4	Buried at Oak Ridge Cemetery outside Springfield, Ill.

TYPESET IN MILLER AND SCOTCH TYPES

Design and typography by Jerry Kelly